THE MYSTERIOUS MULTI

HOW TO PLAY IT HOW TO PLAY AGAINST IT

MASTER POINT PRESS | TORONTO, CANADA

Master Point Press
331 Douglas Ave.
Toronto, Ontario, Canada
M5M 1H2   (416)781-0351
Email: info@masterpointpress.com
Websites: www.masterpointpress.com
                 www.masteringbridge.com
                 www.bridgeblogging.com
                 www.ebooksbridge.com

Library and Archives Canada Cataloguing in Publication

Horton, Mark
        The mysterious multi : how to play it, how to play against it / Mark Horton & Jan van Cleeff.

ISBN 978-1-897106-56-3
        1. Contract bridge—Bidding. I. Title.

GV1282.4.H665 2010   795.41'52   C2009-906754-4

Editor   Ray Lee
Copy editor/interior format   Sally Sparrow
Cover and interior design   Olena S. Sullivan/New Mediatrix

1 2 3 4 5 6 7   14 13 12 11 10

PRINTED IN CANADA

TABLE OF CONTENTS

INTRODUCTION

If you are thinking of playing a convention, perhaps the most critical decision you must make is how serious it will be to give up the meaning of a bid in its natural sense.

In the early days of bridge there were few conventions and the majority of bids were natural. But the language of bidding is one with very few words, and it's important to use those words as efficiently as one can. As the game developed, players began to discover that some natural bids could be put to better use. The classic example is a response of 2♣ to an opening bid of 1NT — the Stayman convention. By the same token, an opening bid at the two-level used to announce possession of a powerful hand. It was many years before someone (Al Roth) realized that weak hands are more frequent than strong ones and introduced the concept of the weak two-bid.

As the game continued to evolve, players with agile minds began to work on the concept of using more and more bids in an artificial way; in particular, the idea that a single bid could encompass various types of hands was intriguing. Combining multiple hand-types into one bid would be efficient, and it would also liberate some other bids for new assignments. That is how the "Multicoloured Two Diamonds" came to be introduced into the game. It soon acquired a new, and simpler, name — the Multi. Once the convention had gained a foothold it became clear that other new ideas would rapidly be developed to make use of the resulting availability of opening bids of 2♡, 2♠ and 2NT.

What we have done in this book is to provide not only a detailed explanation of how to play the Multi, but also a description of many of the associated conventions that have grown up around it. If you want to start playing the Multi, you can select from among these new meanings for your other two-bids, finding something that suits your own style. We have also included chapters on extended 'multi-type' methods, such as the increasingly popular Multi Landy (or Woolsey) defense to 1NT, and the ultra-modern Multi responses to an opening bid of one of a minor.

Even if you don't want to adopt the Multi yourself, you are almost certain to encounter opponents who use it; for you, the material on defending against the Multi will repay study.

Mark Horton, London, September 2009
Jan van Cleeff, The Hague, September 2009

ACKNOWLEDGMENTS

The authors are grateful for material and ideas from the following sources:

Books & Periodicals

Spice Up Your Two-Bids   Brian Senior

Conventions Today   Brian Senior

Preempts from A to Z   Ron Anderson & Sabine Zenkel

The Lebensohl Convention Complete in Contract Bridge
                           Ron Anderson

Bridge Conventions in Depth   Matthew & Pamela Granovetter

Bridge Magazine

Bridge Magazine IMP

Individuals

Tim Bourke, Sally Brock, Bas Drijver, Onno Eskes, Graham Kirby, Eric Kokish, Linda Lee, Ray Lee, Paul Maris, Steve Robinson, Maarten Schollaardt, Kit Woolsey.

CHAPTER 1

HISTORICAL BACKGROUND

It is generally agreed that the birthplace of the Multi 2◇ was England. In order for a convention to be played in UK tournaments, it has to be licensed and approved by the English Bridge Union. It is therefore relatively easy to track down the Multi's first sighting: the EBU Rules and Ethics Committee minutes first mention it in December 1970 in regard to a failed application for a license from Terence Reese. Reese's proposed Multi 2◇ opening showed one of three types of hand: a weak two in a major, a strong balanced hand, or a strong three-suiter. The convention was refused any type of licence by a vote of seven to one. Reese was the first, but by no means was he the only player to try for a license to play the convention — indeed, Mark Horton applied on behalf of a version of his own a short time after this, and like Reese's it was politely refused.

However, the true origin of the concept was probably some years prior to that. Northern Ireland's John Grummit, with help from Jimmy Clarke, devised a convention that he named after the place where he lived — the Holywood Two Diamonds. In the mid 1960s he wrote to Reese to tell him about his invention, and it was probably this letter that eventually led Reese's fertile mind to develop the Multi 2◇.

Others were also working on new systems of two-bids at this time. The classic Acol treatment was to use two-bids for fairly strong, almost game-forcing hands, but these did not occur with great frequency. Meanwhile, weak two-bids were becoming popular, and Albert Benjamin devised a method to combine these with Acol Twos. Multiple meaning bids were also under investigation. In 1968 Hugh Kelsey presented a new idea, Tartan Two-bids, in which an opening bid of 2♡ or 2♠ could be used to describe not only a strong hand in the original Acol style, but also a weak two-suited hand.

While Tartan Twos never gained a huge following, largely owing to their complexity, Benjamin Twos and the Multi 2◇ quickly did so. Even in the aftermath of the Buenos Aires cheating scandal, Reese was still regarded as one of the world's best players and writers, and with his name behind it the Multi 2◇ became very popular in the UK. Reese himself introduced it into international play in partnership with Jeremy Flint. For a long time opponents did not know how to cope with it as they were unsure whether a weak or strong hand was lurking behind the 2◇ opening. This lack of any effective defensive methods meant that early proponents of the Multi obtained a disproportionate number of good results, adding to its allure.

The first reference we can find to the convention appearing in top-level play is at the 1970 European Championships in Estoril. This deal illustrates the inability of the opponents to get into the auction using the methods available to them at the time.

In Round 9, Great Britain faced Norway:

N-S vul.

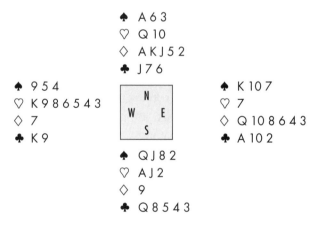

```
              ♠ A 6 3
              ♡ Q 10
              ◇ A K J 5 2
              ♣ J 7 6
  ♠ 9 5 4            N            ♠ K 10 7
  ♡ K 9 8 6 5 4 3  W   E          ♡ 7
  ◇ 7                 S           ◇ Q 10 8 6 4 3
  ♣ K 9                           ♣ A 10 2
              ♠ Q J 8 2
              ♡ A J 2
              ◇ 9
              ♣ Q 8 5 4 3
```

West	North	East	South
Reese		*Flint*	
2◇*	pass	2♡[1]	pass
pass	3◇	all pass	

1. Pass or correct.

As you will see, today's experts have no problem getting into the auction on North's hand. In 1970, North had no obvious action and South felt that his partner's hand was limited by his initial pass. The 3◇ contract went three down while at the other table North-South bid and made 3NT after West had opened a 'normal' 2♡.

However things were not always so rosy, as illustrated by this deal from Great Britain's match against Belgium in Round 10. Constructive bidding over the Multi had yet to be refined, and it was already clear that the marriage of weak and strong hand types had some intrinsic issues.

N-S vul.

♠ A J 4 3		♠ K Q 10 5
♡ J 8 4		♡ A K 10 7 5
♢ 8 6 5 4		♢ —
♣ 6 4		♣ A K 10 3

West	**North**	**East**	**South**
Pugh		*Gordon*	
		2♢*	pass
2♡[1]	pass	3♣[2]	pass
4♠	all pass		

1. Pass or correct.
2. Strong three-suiter.

West had the machinery to discover East's exact shape, but didn't use it (presumably not envisaging a slam opposite his hand) and the excellent 6♠ contract was missed.

Any time you adopt complex new methods, there is potential for disaster. That's what happened here in the match against Israel in Round 15 of the same event:

E-W vul.

```
        ♠ Q 9 8 5 2                      ♠ A K 10 7
        ♡ 8 7 5 4          N             ♡ A Q 10 3
        ◇ A 8          W       E         ◇ K 10 7 2
        ♣ A 7              S             ♣ K
```

West	North	East	South
Reese		*Flint*	
pass	pass	2◇*	pass
2NT¹	pass	3♠*	pass
4♠	all pass		

1. Forcing relay.

Flint's rebid of 3♠ purported to show a minimum weak 2♠ opener — in an unusual lapse of concentration he simply made the wrong response. Flint, reporting in *Bridge Magazine,* observed later that once he was in the bunker he had no sand wedge available. He could hardly bid on over 4♠ as West might have had two small spades.

Of course, this particular example does not demonstrate a flaw in the Multi itself, but highlights an issue that occurs with any new convention: that of remembering what the various bids mean. When Sandra Landy, who in those days was partnering Nicola Gardener on the British women's team, suggested that they incorporate it into their system, Nicola declared it far too complicated to remember. Undaunted, Sandra suggested a modification whereby a sequence such as 2◇-2♡-3♣ would show an Acol Two-bid. She ran this past Jeremy Flint and, when he agreed it was a reasonable idea, it was refined with the help of another Acol guru, Eric Crowhurst. The result was that the Multi was incorporated into the Smith-Landy methods in time for the European championships in 1977.

In 1972 Reese's book on the Precision Club was published but it made no mention of the Multi — the convention was still without an EBU license. However, Reese and Flint took part in the Deauville Tournament of Champions in that same year and this deal showed that there was still much work to be done on both sides of the table:

N-S vul.

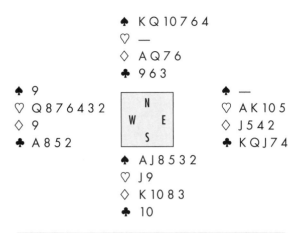

♠ K Q 10 7 6 4
♡ —
◇ A Q 7 6
♣ 9 6 3

♠ 9
♡ Q 8 7 6 4 3 2
◇ 9
♣ A 8 5 2

♠ —
♡ A K 10 5
◇ J 5 4 2
♣ K Q J 7 4

♠ A J 8 5 3 2
♡ J 9
◇ K 10 8 3
♣ 10

West	North	East	South
Sharif	*Reese*	*Sussel*	*Flint*
			2◇*
2♡	2♠	3♠[1]	pass
4♡	all pass		

1. Game force with heart support.

With twelve tricks available to North-South in spades (or at least a small plus against the 7♡ sacrifice), an East-West game making with overtricks was hardly the ideal result for our heroes. It was suggested that Flint thought Reese's 2♠ bid was an attempt to sow confusion — if so, it certainly worked!

There is plenty of evidence to suggest that the best way to defend against the Multi was yet to be established. Our own favorite story concerns a club player holding a terrific three-suited hand with a void in spades. When RHO opened a Multi 2◇, he overcalled with 2♠, expecting his partner to recognise it as a takeout of spades. His partner, holding a singleton spade, saw things differently and passed.

When the time came to score up the following exchange took place:

'Minus 50. Sorry, I went down in 7◇, though I could have made it.'
'Push.'
'Oh, they went down in 7◇ as well?'
'No, they were one down in 2♠.'

But even among top experts it was easy enough to go wrong, as this deal from the 1972 Deauville event illustrates:

E-W vul.

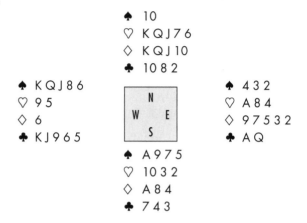

```
              ♠ 10
              ♡ K Q J 7 6
              ◇ K Q J 10
              ♣ 10 8 2
♠ K Q J 8 6              ♠ 4 3 2
♡ 9 5          N        ♡ A 8 4
◇ 6        W     E      ◇ 9 7 5 3 2
♣ K J 9 6 5    S        ♣ A Q
              ♠ A 9 7 5
              ♡ 10 3 2
              ◇ A 8 4
              ♣ 7 4 3
```

West	North	East	South
Flint	Carcy	Reese	Calix
		pass	pass
2◇*	dbl	2NT[1]	dbl
3♠	pass	pass	dbl
all pass			

1. Forcing relay.

Here, it seems that North-South did not have sufficiently clear agreements on the strength shown by the various doubles. North led the ♡K against 3♠, doubled, and declarer was not hard pressed to make ten tricks for +930.

There was further evidence of defensive uncertainty when England met Scotland later that same year in the Camrose Trophy:

Both vul.

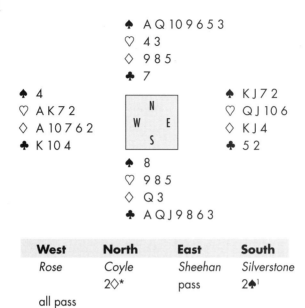

♠ A Q 10 9 6 5 3
♡ 4 3
◇ 9 8 5
♣ 7

♠ 4
♡ A K 7 2
◇ A 10 7 6 2
♣ K 10 4

♠ K J 7 2
♡ Q J 10 6
◇ K J 4
♣ 5 2

♠ 8
♡ 9 8 5
◇ Q 3
♣ A Q J 9 8 6 3

West	North	East	South
Rose	Coyle	Sheehan	Silverstone
	2◇*	pass	2♠[1]
all pass			

1. To play opposite a weak two in spades.

It seems odd that West allowed the auction to die in 2♠, but perhaps he was misled by South's implied preference for hearts. Declarer went two down for –200, but in the other room East-West recorded eleven tricks in 3NT.

The Multi 2◇ was finally given a restricted English Bridge Union licence in 1974 under somewhat dubious circumstances. A tediously long Rules and Ethics Committee meeting on December 4th had failed to complete its agenda, and the eight members present agreed to adjourn the meeting until December 19th. Not surprisingly, due to the proximity of the holidays, the attendance was poor at the second session. Bypassing the usual formal proposal and acceptance process, those present agreed the following by a 3-1 vote:

"*Multicoloured Two Diamonds opening bid*

In view of the numbers of applications received for the licensing of this bid, the fact that it is now widely played in international events, and the amount of publicity which it has received, the committee decided on its own initiative to give it an 'A' licence for a strictly limited period until the 31st December, 1975."

The convention as licensed covered three types of holdings:
* *A weak two-bid in the majors.*
* *A balanced hand of either above or below a 2NT opening bid, by decision of the partnership.*
* *A Roman 2♦ type, with 4-4-4-1 shape, with 17-20 points if the singleton is in the minor suit and with 21-23 points if the singleton is in the major suit.*

The 'temporary' licence has never been revoked, but has been amended to allow the 2♦ opening to include other types of hand, including:
* *A one-suiter — 11 to 14 points*
* *A one-suited Acol two-bid*
* *A Flannery-type two-suiter — 17 + points*

In April 1976 the same committee asked Chris Dixon to write an article on defending against the Multi for the May *EBU Quarterly*. The Dixon defense remains one of the most popular in the United Kingdom (you will find it in Chapter 4).

One weakness of the full-blown Multi is the inability of responder to raise the level of the preempt without a fit for both majors, allied to the problems that a jump might cause if the opening includes a strong option. This resulted in the development of a version of the Multi that only incorporates a weak two in a major, which today is perhaps the commonest version of the convention encountered in expert play.

As you will discover later in the book, the modern player has a range of effective defenses from which to choose, and the Multi today no longer terrorizes the opposition as it did when first introduced. Likewise, opening a preemptive spade hand with 2♦ affords the opponents an easy natural 2♥ overcall if their methods allow it. However, some of its advantages remain intact, in particular the fact that the opening bids of 2♥ and 2♠ (and possibly even 2NT) can be freed up for other uses, while a typical weak two-bid hand in a major suit is opened 2♦.

As with any convention, there are trade-offs. Every partnership will have to decide for itself whether there is a net gain from incorporating the Multi 2♦ into its methods.

CHAPTER 2

THE BASICS OF THE MULTI 2♢

In its original form, the Multi 2♢ was seen as a constructive rather than destructive weapon. Perhaps the greatest gain was that by using a single opening bid to combine weak two-bids and certain less frequent strong hand types, opening bids of 2♡ and 2♠ could be used to describe different types of hand. If you include a strong balanced hand in your Multi scheme, the opening 2NT bid is also released. As you will see later on in this book, there is no shortage of ideas as to how these bids might profitably be employed.

THE OPENING 2♢ BID

There are various ways to treat the opening 2♢ bid, depending on which hand types you wish to include. In Europe one has pretty much a free choice, but in North America one's options are limited.

Reese's earliest version promised either:
* *A weak two-bid in a major, or*
* *A strong balanced hand, or*
* *A strong 4-4-4-1 hand*

Later versions replaced the three-suited option with a strong two-bid in a minor.

Let's look more closely at the kinds of hands included in each of these possibilities.

A WEAK TWO-BID IN A MAJOR

The following discussion applies whether or not you decide to start playing a Multi 2◇. Any partnership playing weak twos has to have some agreements on

* *Suit quality*
* *Suit length*
* *Point range*

including how these can vary with vulnerability.

Suppose you as responder know your partner has a weak two in spades and you have a hand which includes ♠A5. If partner's suit is ♠KQJ743 or ♠KQ10642 (or even ♠KJ10862) there are chances of six tricks. However if partner's suit can be as weak as ♠J98742 then that possibility flies out of the window. This is important when you are thinking in terms of a possible game and even more so if you are considering a slam.

With that in mind, you should have some agreement about the quality of your suit. For example, in first or second positions you might agree that it must contain two of the top four honors. Or you might decide that even something like ♡K108752 is good enough. Another question to resolve is whether the suit can be as good as ♠AKQ874. In third position you might adopt a more freewheeling approach, as the chances of a constructive auction have diminished and you are usually trying to be disruptive. What is important is to have some agreement, even if you take the macho approach that anything goes in any position and whatever the vulnerability.

To try and get a feel for this, let's look at some examples of hands that were opened with a Multi 2◇ in expert competition — this particular batch all come from the 2005 World Championships in Estoril.

Vul. vs. not vul.

♠A Q 10 9 4 2   ♡7 3   ◇6 5   ♣K 8 4

A classic weak two-bid.

Vul. vs. not vul.

♠ —   ♡A 10 9 7 5 4   ◇6 4 3 2   ♣K J 5

The excellent shape makes this a sound proposition, although you might prefer those club honors to be in diamonds.

Not vul. vs. vul.

♠ K J 6 5 4 3   ♡ Q 9 7   ◇ 8 2   ♣ J 7

Not much of a suit but the vulnerability is in your favor.

Vul. vs. not vul.

♠ K J 10 5 3 2   ♡ Q 3   ◇ J 2   ♣ 6 4 2

The ♠10 makes all the difference to this hand.

Vul. vs. not vul.

♠ A K Q 8 4 3   ♡ 9 8 6   ◇ 10 8 5   ♣ 9

Every partnership should discuss whether this particular holding is a possibility.

Vul. vs. not vul.

♠ A K 10 9 8 4   ♡ Q 10 3   ◇ 8 7   ♣ 9 2

Another sound weak two-bid.

Not vul. vs. vul.

♠ Q 5   ♡ J 9 8 6 5 4   ◇ J 5   ♣ Q 10 8

Well, we wouldn't open this, but you might.

Not vul. vs. vul.

♠ 3   ♡ K Q 9 6 5   ◇ 10 9 8 7 5   ♣ K 9

Only a five-card suit, but good distribution (again with a misplaced side honor) and favorable vulnerability. In Chapter 5 of this book you will see an alternative (and perhaps superior) method that allows you to open this hand without blushing.

Both vul.

♠ K Q 8 6 5 4   ♡ 8 4 2   ◇ 8 7 5   ♣ 2

A reasonable suit and a distributional feature.

Both vul.

♠ 8 4　♡ K Q 9 8 6 3　♢ 8 7　♣ 8 4 3

Much the same as the hand above, but no singleton.

Both vul.

♠ 9 3　♡ K Q J 7 6 4 3　♢ 8 7　♣ 4 3

The vulnerability and the sterile 2-7-2-2 shape argue against a more aggressive 3♡ opening.

As you can see from these examples, the suit quality can vary quite considerably: from AKQ843 to J98654 (and we have seen worse than that). Although we think that having some minimum requirements as to suit quality for first and second chair openings gives you a better chance of bidding constructively, it is possible to adopt the all-in approach, taking the view that when you have a weak hand your primary objective is to disrupt the opponents' auction.

We mentioned that the number of cards in your suit may vary, and the above examples included both seven- and five-card suits. Again, your partnership needs to have an agreement on whether such variances from the 'norm' are allowed.

The other major question surrounds the number of points your weak two should contain. Looking at the above examples you see hands ranging from 5 to 9 HCP. That strikes us as being about dead center, but you may prefer something else — certainly with a lower starting point, but not much higher, as by the time you have 10 points and a six-card major you are close to a real opening bid.

As we mentioned earlier, the latest versions of the Multi are *weak only* — by no means a bad idea as it sometimes allows for more vigorous preemption.

STRONG BALANCED HANDS

Having taken care of the weak option, let's look at the strong balanced type, the equivalent of a 2NT opening bid, promising whatever range you consider appropriate — we'll use 20-22 HCP. Here, vulnerability is not an issue.

♠ A Q 7 4 ♡ K J 5 ◇ A K 7 ♣ A J 10

An absolute maximum.

♠ K 7 3 ♡ A 6 ◇ K 10 ♣ A K Q J 7 5

A minimum in terms of high card points, but with significantly greater playing strength that the previous hand.

♠ A 8 ♡ K J 10 7 5 ◇ A Q J ♣ K Q 6

A five-card major is no bar to opening 2NT; nor does it prevent you from opening 2◇.

STRONG THREE-SUITED HANDS

The classical strong three-suiter is any 4-4-4-1 with 17-24 points, as in the Blue Team Club system. It's important to have quite a high minimum HCP requirement, otherwise you may find yourself uncomfortably high when responder has a very weak hand.

Here are some examples:

♠ A K J 5 ♡ K J 4 2 ◇ 6 ♣ K Q 10 7

A minimum hand.

♠ K Q J 7 ♡ 8 ◇ A K Q 4 ♣ A K Q 6

A perfect maximum.

♠ K J 8 5 ♡ A ◇ K Q 10 7 ♣ K J 6 3

A minimum including a singleton ace — we would open this 1♣ or 1◇.

♠ K Q J 7 ♡ A K Q 5 ◇ A ♣ A 8 7 4

With a maximum a singleton ace is no bar to opening 2◇.

♠ A Q 6 4 ♡ A K Q 7 ◇ — ♣ A K Q 6 4

If you open 2◇ with this monster, there is no way to show the void at an economical level so it's much better to open 2♣.

ACOL TWO IN A MINOR

In the original Acol system a two-bid was expected to have at least eight playing tricks. Here are some examples.

♠ 9 6 ♡ A J 4 ◇ 5 ♣ A K Q 8 7 5 3

Although the club suit is not solid there is a reasonable prospect of eight tricks.

♠ A K 5 ♡ 6 ◇ K Q J 10 9 7 4 ♣ K 5

This time eight tricks are certain.

♠ 7 ♡ A K 9 8 6 ◇ A Q J 10 5 4 ♣ 3

Two-suited hands are awkward as the space used up by opening at the two-level makes it difficult to show both suits. On this type of hand it's much better to open 1◇ and bid hearts on the next round.

In summary

A partnership has to decide which version of the Multi to adopt:
*   *Weak Two only (as favored by Jeff Meckstroth and Eric Rodwell)*
*   *Weak Two plus strong balanced hand*
*   *Weak Two plus strong balanced hand and strong three-suiter*
*   *Weak Two plus strong balanced hand and strong twos in a minor*

As strong twos and powerful three-suiters are somewhat rare, we prefer the second version, which has the merit of making the 2NT opening bid available to show a weak minor two-suiter.

RESPONDING TO 2◇

Whatever your agreements regarding the inclusion of strong hands, responder initially assumes that the Multi 2◇ opening is based on a weak two-bid in major. Presented here is our own choice of a response structure. It is (relatively) simple, and quite effective. If you want to get sophisticated, there are plenty of more complex ideas in Chapter 3.

Like everyone else, we prefer to use 2NT as a forcing inquiry, while keeping most major-suit bids as 'pass or correct'. That leaves minor-suit responses at the three- and four-level undefined, and available for assignment. Here's a summary of the structure:

2◇ – ?

2♡	Pass or correct
2♠	Pass or correct
2NT	Forcing, asks for more information
3♣	Natural, forcing
3◇	Natural, forcing
3♡	Pass or correct
3♠	Natural, invitational
3NT	To play
4♣	Transfer to opener's major
4◇	Transfer to opener's major, no slam interest
4♡	To play
4♠	To play

Even within this structure, there are some options, so let's look at each of the possible responses in detail, and see how the auction develops subsequently. For the moment we will assume that you are using our suggested option of a two-way Multi, with weak twos and a strong balanced hand in the range of 20-22. (We'll look at what happens when strong two-bids or three-suiters are included later.)

If your Multi does not include strong hands, you will find that the rebids showing that option can just be eliminated. It's also worth pointing out that some regulating authorities have introduced rules that compel you to respond constructively to an opening 2◇ with any minimal values on the basis that you should explore reasonable game possibilities opposite a strong hand type. One way of getting round this is to play in the style of Meckwell and include no strong option; another is to have only one — a solid-suit Acol Two-bid in diamonds! (A cunning idea developed by England's Jeffrey Allerton to outflank the lawmakers.)

2◇-2♡

Pass or correct. Opener passes with a weak two in hearts or corrects to 2♠. Responder might have one of these hands:

♠ K J 5	♠ Q 6 3
♡ 8 4	♡ 7 4
◇ Q 9 7 3	◇ A 10 6 4
♣ 10 9 8 4	♣ A K 8 3

Responder may also bid 2♡ on a hand where he has good support for spades and intends to go on if opener rebids 2♠. For example:

♠ K 8 7 4   ♡ 7   ◇ A Q 8 3 2   ♣ A 7 3

Opener has three possible rebids:
* *With a weak two in hearts opener passes*
* *With a weak two in spades, opener bids 2♠*
* *With a balanced 20-22 opener rebids 2NT. Thereafter a normal structure can be employed: Stayman, transfers, etc., etc.*

2◇-2♠

This shows a hand which does not wish to go beyond 2♠ if opener has a weak two in spades, but has reasonable support for hearts, and may be intending to bid on if opener rebids 3♡. With this hand:

♠ 8 3   ♡ K 10 6   ◇ Q 8 4 2   ♣ J 9 5 3

responder intends to pass a rebid of 3♡.

♠ 7 4   ♡ Q 9 6 3   ◇ A J 5   ♣ A K 10 6

This time responder will raise a rebid of 3♡ to game.

There are four possibilities for opener's rebid:

* *With a weak two in spades, opener passes.*
* *With a weak two in hearts, opener rebids 3♡.*
* *You can also play that with a minimum weak two in hearts opener rebids 3♡, and with a maximum opener rebids 4♡.*

Remember that the 2♠ response has implied a willingness to play at the three-level in hearts. However, adopting this approach reduces your options in preemptive situations. Give responder

♠ 5   ♡ K 4 2   ◇ 9 5 3 2   ♣ K 6 4 3 2

and he will want to raise a weak 2♡ to 3♡, certainly at favorable vulnerability. So over an opening 2◇, 2♠ is the obvious response, but responder really has no desire to have opener jump to 4♡ on a 'good' weak two. You can't have it both ways — if you allow opener to rebid 4♡ over 2♠, you must be more careful when you use that response.

A possible improvement once partner has responded 2♠ and opener has a heart suit is to rebid as one would over a 2NT inquiry response to a standard weak two-bid. This is one scheme, developed by Harold Ogust, which only rarely commits the partnership beyond the three-level in opener's major:

3♣	Minimum points with a poor heart suit
3◇	Maximum points with a poor heart suit
3♡	Minimum points with a good heart suit
3♠	Maximum points with a good heart suit
3NT	A solid heart suit

One way to remember these responses is use the reminder P (points) before Q (suit quality).

As we mentioned earlier, the definition of a good suit is something that you and your partner have to agree on. For instance, in the example hands quoted above, is ♡KJ10742 a poor suit or a good one? (We would say good, whereas ♡QJ10742 would be poor, but this is a matter for discussion.)

* *With 20-22 opener rebids 2NT, and a normal structure applies thereafter.*

The 2NT Inquiry

This is a forcing response showing at least game interest in at least one major opposite a weak two. In terms of points, there is no hard and fast rule, but 15+ is a reasonable guide. The 2NT response preserves more space than an immediate response of 4♣ or 4◇, which may be useful if opener happens to have a strong hand.

A question that is frequently asked is which game responder should be looking for, 3NT or four of a major. There can be no hard and fast rule, but on marginal hands if you can establish that the major-suit fit is likely to deliver six tricks, then 3NT is usually the right spot. Otherwise it tends to be better to play in the major suit, even though this means you need an extra trick.

We think this is the best scheme to adopt over the 2NT inquiry:

2◇ – 2NT	*Invitational (or better) relay*		
?			
3♣	*Bad/intermediate weak two in hearts*		
	3◇	*Asks*	
		3♡ = *bad weak two in hearts*	
		3♠ = *intermediate weak two in hearts*	
	3♡	*To play*	
	3♠	*Good suit, forcing*	
	3NT	*To play*	
3◇	*Bad/intermediate weak two in spades*		
	3♡	*Asks*	
		3♠ = *bad weak two in spades*	
		3NT = *intermediate weak two in spades*	
	3♠	*To play*	
	3NT	*To play*	
3♡	*Good weak two in spades*		
3♠	*Good weak two in hearts*		
3NT	*AKQxxx in either major*		
4NT	*20-22 balanced*		

This scheme of rebidding has two important advantages:
* *the final contract is right-sided more frequently*
* *you have a huge degree of flexibility as three types of weak twos can be covered: bad/intermediate/good*

By using 3♡ and 3♠ to show the maximum hands you get more room to explore slam possibilities. The inversion of these responses (bidding 3♡ with spades and 3♠ with hearts) is a little harder to remember, but conceals the strong hand during the play, so is slightly better theoretically. (As an aside, we recall that in days gone by one of the authors, when partnering Brian Senior, agreed that the sequence 2◇-2NT-3♠ simply said 'I apologize for opening my hand.') If opener shows a minimum hand then responder may elect to pass.

We'll examine some more complex methods of replying to 2NT later on. Meanwhile, let's look at some hands on which you would respond 2NT.

♠ K Q 7 4 ♡ A J 5 3 2 ◇ 9 ♣ A J 3

Once responder knows which major partner has he will go on to game in that major. An alternative approach would be to use either 4♣ or 4◇, but that might create a minor problem if partner had 20-22, as his response of 4NT would eliminate the possibility of using Blackwood and there might just be an ace missing.

♠ A J 6 ♡ K 10 5 2 ◇ A 10 4 2 ♣ A J

A slightly stronger hand but again responder intends to raise to game once he has discovered which major opener has. This example is very close to being worth a slam try, but facing something along the lines of

♠ 6 ♡ A J 9 8 6 4 ◇ K J 5 ♣ 8 7 3

the heart slam is not a laydown.

♠ K 10 6 4 ♡ A J 7 ◇ A K ♣ A K 8 6

Here responder intends to make a slam try.

Now let's look at some examples where you need to find out more about partner's hand to decide how high to bid. You have:

♠ A 5 ♡ 8 5 4 ♢ A Q 7 2 ♣ K Q 10 4

Partner opens 2♢, Multi. Is the hand worth a game try?
Yes. Opposite a **strong** or an **intermediate** weak two, game must have good chances. However, if partner has a **bad** weak two, you don't want to be so high, so make an inquiry with 2NT.
When opener has:

♠ K Q 10 6 4 3 ♡ A 2 ♢ 6 3 ♣ 7 5 2

he will rebid 3♡, showing a **good** weak two in spades. And you will raise to 4♠.
When opener has:

♠ Q 10 9 6 4 3 ♡ A 2 ♢ 6 3 ♣ 7 5 2

he will rebid 3♢, showing a **bad** or **intermediate** weak two in spades. Now you bid 3♡, and opener, with his bad weak two, signs off in 3♠.
When opener has:

♠ K J 10 6 4 3 ♡ A 2 ♢ 6 3 ♣ 7 5 2

he will rebid 3♢, showing a **bad** or **intermediate** weak two in spades. Now you bid 3♡ — a "Last Train" game try — to which opener, with his intermediate weak two, bids 3NT in order to right-side the contract. And then you correct to 4♠.
When you have a stronger hand you can try for a slam. Suppose you have, for instance:

♠ A 5 ♡ K J 4 ♢ A K 7 2 ♣ K Q 10 4

Opener	You
2♢	2NT
3♡	?

the best bid here is a simple 3♠ (forcing of course). This gives opener space to do something intelligent. With:

$$\spadesuit K Q 10 6 4 3 \quad \heartsuit A 2 \quad \diamondsuit 6 3 \quad \clubsuit 7 5 2$$

he will bid 4$\heartsuit$, a cuebid denying controls in clubs and diamonds, and you will ask for keycards. So:

Opener	RHO	You	LHO
2$\diamondsuit$	pass	2NT	pass
3$\heartsuit$[1]	pass	3$\spadesuit$	pass
4$\heartsuit$[2]	pass	4NT[3]	pass
5$\clubsuit$[4]	pass	6$\spadesuit$	all pass

1. Good weak two in spades.
2. Cuebid.
3. RKCB.
4. 2 keycards + trump queen.

2$\diamondsuit$-3$\clubsuit$ and 2$\diamondsuit$-3$\diamondsuit$

These bids are both natural and forcing, and opener will normally now show his suit.

$$\spadesuit 6 4 \quad \heartsuit K 10 4 \quad \diamondsuit A Q \quad \clubsuit A K Q 9 6 4$$

Here responder starts with 3$\clubsuit$, intending to raise 3$\heartsuit$ to game and bid 3NT over 3$\spadesuit$.

$$\spadesuit Q 9 4 \quad \heartsuit A \quad \diamondsuit A K J 10 8 7 \quad \clubsuit K J 10$$

This time responder, having bid 3$\diamondsuit$, will bid 3NT over 3$\heartsuit$ and go on to 4$\spadesuit$ over 3$\spadesuit$.

Sometimes opener has excellent support for partner:

$$\spadesuit 6 \quad \heartsuit A J 10 7 3 2 \quad \diamondsuit 8 4 \quad \clubsuit K 10 7 4$$

Rebid 4$\clubsuit$ over 3$\clubsuit$, but rebid 3$\heartsuit$ over 3$\diamondsuit$.

♠KQJ854 ♡754 ◇K8 ♣93

Here you should rebid 3♠ over 3♣ or 3◇ unless you have an agreement that with a maximum you should jump to game in your major.

With 20-22 opener rebids 3NT. Of course, responder may still be interested in a major-suit game, and your normal 2NT opening structure should apply.

2◇-3♡

This is a preemptive response based on a weak hand with support for both majors. This hand is a good example:

♠K1042 ♡QJ743 ◇82 ♣64

You would like to jump to four of whichever major partner has, but if you bid 4◇, partner might just have a balanced 20-22 and 4NT might well be both too high and the wrong contract. Our view is that this is a small price to pay. However, if you so wish you can avoid it by using a weak-only Multi along with the responses outlined in Chapter 3.

Over a 3♡ response, opener passes with a weak two in hearts, bids 3♠ with spades, or 3NT with 20-22.

2◇-3♠

In the early days of the Multi this was played as a limit bid. The message it conveyed was that if opener had a weak two in spades this was as high as responder was prepared to go, but if the weak two was in hearts then responder's hand was suitable for game. The passage of time has suggested that the bid is better used as a natural invitational bid, for example with:

♠AKJ1074 ♡8 ◇QJ5 ♣A104

Over this natural and invitational bid opener has five possibilities:
* *Pass with a modest hand*

♠73 ♡Q109542 ◇K83 ♣J7

* *Raise to 4♠ with support*

♠ Q 7 4   ♡ K J 10 8 5 4   ◇ 8 4 2   ♣ 7

* *Cuebid in support of spades (on this hand, 4♣).*

♠ Q 9 3   ♡ A K 10 7 3 2   ◇ 10 9 4   ♣ 6

* *Rebid 4♡ with good hearts and a good hand.*

♠ 8 2   ♡ K Q 10 9 8 3   ◇ 9 3   ♣ K 7 3

* *Rebid 3NT to show 20-22.*

♠ K 9 4   ♡ A Q 10 4   ◇ K Q J 4   ♣ A J

Of course, you *can* also treat 2◇-3♠ as a pass or correct sequence, analogous to 2◇-2♠. It's consistent and therefore easier to remember, but not quite as efficient.

2◇-3NT

This is to play facing a weak two-bid, usually being based on a long-running minor. (In the version originally played by Reese & Flint it promised a powerful minor two-suiter with around four losers, but that has fallen into disuse.)

♠ A 6   ♡ K 7   ◇ 10 5   ♣ A K Q J 8 7 4

Opener obviously passes unless he happens to have 20-22. In that case one option is for opener to respond to 3NT as if it were Blackwood, another to bid 4NT (after which 5♣ should ask for aces). A more obscure possibility would be to bid 4♣ with 20 points, 4◇ with 21 points and 4♡ with 22 points, after which 4NT should be Blackwood. Simpler souls might just jump to 7NT on this hand once they know partner has the strong balanced type.

There are various ways in which this bid might be used. A straightforward meaning would be as a request for opener to bid game in his major suit (assuming he has a weak two). It might also be used to show a powerful two-suited hand. You might also use the bid to show a preemptive raise with support for both majors. The method we prefer is for it to set up a transfer, which enables responder to become declarer. Opener bids 4◇ with hearts or 4♡ with spades and then responder will either choose the final contract or make some forward-going move on a hand where he has some slam interest. The theoretical advantage is that responder's hand remains hidden.

Here is an illustration from the 2008 World Bridge Games in Beijing:

Both vul.

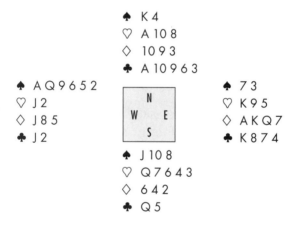

	♠ K 4	
	♡ A 10 8	
	◇ 10 9 3	
	♣ A 10 9 6 3	
♠ A Q 9 6 5 2		♠ 7 3
♡ J 2		♡ K 9 5
◇ J 8 5		◇ A K Q 7
♣ J 2		♣ K 8 7 4
	♠ J 10 8	
	♡ Q 7 6 4 3	
	◇ 6 4 2	
	♣ Q 5	

West	North	East	South
H. Wang	Senior	Sun	Dhondy
2◇*	pass	4♣[1]	pass
4♡[2]	pass	4♠	all pass

1. Tell me your suit.
2. Spades.

It is clearly best for East to be declarer in order to avoid a potentially awkward lead.

2◇-4◇

This asks opener to bid his major suit and shows no slam interest; for example responder might have:

♠ Q 10 4   ♡ J 9 6 3   ◇ A 10   ♣ A K Q 5

Here is an example from the 2006 Women's World Pairs Championship in Verona:

N-S vul.

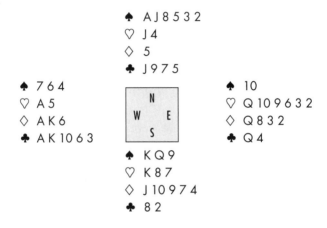

	♠ A J 8 5 3 2	
	♡ J 4	
	◇ 5	
	♣ J 9 7 5	
♠ 7 6 4		♠ 10
♡ A 5		♡ Q 10 9 6 3 2
◇ A K 6		◇ Q 8 3 2
♣ A K 10 6 3		♣ Q 4
	♠ K Q 9	
	♡ K 8 7	
	◇ J 10 9 7 4	
	♣ 8 2	

West	North	East	South
Ponomareva	*Sver*	*Gromova*	*Pilipovic*
		2◇*	pass
4◇[1]	pass	4♡	all pass

1. Bid your suit please.

Obviously, opener would rebid 4NT with 20-22.

2◇-4♡ and 2◇-4♠

These responses are to play:

♠6 ♡AKJ10874 ◇KJ43 ♣9

Opener should only bid on with 20-22 balanced. You could agree that after 2◇-4♡, 4♠ showed the big balanced hand, or that it was a cuebid in support of hearts (with 4NT being RKCB). Similarly, you might agree that after 2◇-4♠, 4NT was Blackwood for spades and that alternatives were cuebids in support of spades.

If you decide to dispense with the responses of 4♣ and 4◇ as transfers then you can play 4♡ as a pass-or-correct preemptive bid, to play in partner's major.

Pass: the rarest action by responder

There is one response we have not mentioned:

Opener	Responder
2◇	pass!

If your Multi includes a strong option this obviously entails some risk, but if responder has a hand like:

♠64 ♡8 ◇Q1098652 ♣J53

or

♠6 ♡74 ◇Q97532 ♣A642

then it may have some merit even then.

OTHER STRONG OPTIONS

There are two more sets of rebids to consider for those who want to include an Acol two-bid in a minor or a strong three-suiter as options for their 2◇ opening.

Acol two-bid in a minor

After 2◇-2M, opener can rebid 3♣ or 3◇ to show his suit.

After 2◇-2NT opener rebids as follows:

3♣	*Weak two in hearts*
3◇	*Weak two in spades*
3♡	*Strong two in clubs*
3♠	*Strong two in diamonds*

Over 3♣/3◇ responder can use the next suit as a relay to ask opener if he is better than minimum.

Strong three-suiter

After 2◇-2M opener bids three of a suit to show 17-24 with a shortage in the suit above the one he has bid:

3♣	*Singleton diamond*
3◇	*Singleton heart*
3♡	*Singleton spade (over 2◇-2♡ only)*
3♠	*Singleton club*

The exception is that after 2◇-2♠ opener has to be able to bid 3♡ with a minimum weak two in that suit, so 3NT is used to show a 1-4-4-4 hand.

Once the singleton is known responder can use a bid of the known short suit to ask for more information — either range or controls. However, Acol two-bids and strong three-suited hands are comparatively rare and in our view do not justify the effort required to memorize the complex responses involved. It is better to stick to a weak-only version or one which only includes a strong balanced hand.

INTERFERENCE OVER 2◇

As an opening 2◇ will generally be based on a weak two-bid one can expect the opponents to get into the auction a fair percentage of the time. When they do, responder has to overcome the fact that opener's suit is unknown.

An immediate double

This takes away no bidding space, so in principle we can use the same set of responses that we have already outlined. However, we also have two new possibilities, pass and redouble, and these can be used advantageously.

Pass can be used to suggest a hand that is playable in diamonds — probably at least a five-card suit — and although opener is free to bid his own suit (assuming he is weak) there is no harm in giving yourself an extra opportunity to find a playable spot.

Here is a perfect example from the 2009 Turkish Team Championship:

E-W vul.

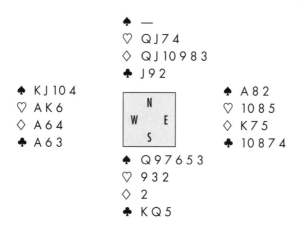

```
              ♠ —
              ♡ Q J 7 4
              ◇ Q J 10 9 8 3
              ♣ J 9 2
♠ K J 10 4           N           ♠ A 8 2
♡ A K 6                          ♡ 10 8 5
◇ A 6 4        W         E       ◇ K 7 5
♣ A 6 3              S           ♣ 10 8 7 4
              ♠ Q 9 7 6 5 3
              ♡ 9 3 2
              ◇ 2
              ♣ K Q 5
```

West	North	East	South
Vahabogl	Tokay	Aydogdu	Kubac
		pass	2◇*
dbl	pass*	2NT	pass
3NT	all pass		

East-West were not getting rich defending 2◊ doubled, but 2♠ doubled might have been a different story.

Redouble might be used to show a good hand, but since you have to allow for the possibility of the final contract being 2◊ redoubled it follows that you must also have length in diamonds. That decreases your chances of being able to double any contract that the opponents might bid. Another possibility is to use the bid simply to ask opener to bid his suit. It may be even better to use the bid as a relay, asking opener to rebid 2♡; after that responder sets the final contract, either passing or bidding another suit.

We can summarize this in the following table of bids:

West	North	East	South
2◊	(dbl)	?	

pass   *Suggests playing in diamonds*
redbl *Relay to 2♡, to play in responder's own suit (which might be hearts)*
2♡   *To play opposite a weak two in hearts*
2♠   *To play opposite a weak two in spades, but forward-going opposite hearts*
2NT   *Forcing inquiry*
3♣   *Natural and forcing*
3◊   *Natural and forcing*
3♡   *Preemptive in partner's major*
3♠   *Natural and invitational*

Here is an example of responder using the 2♡ bid after a double, from the 2007 World Transnational Open Teams in Shanghai:

Both vul.

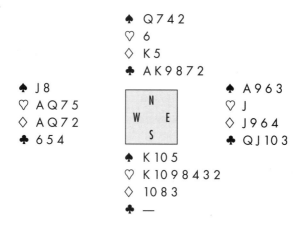

	♠ Q 7 4 2	
	♡ 6	
	◇ K 5	
	♣ A K 9 8 7 2	

♠ J 8		♠ A 9 6 3
♡ A Q 7 5	N	♡ J
◇ A Q 7 2	W E	◇ J 9 6 4
♣ 6 5 4	S	♣ Q J 10 3

	♠ K 10 5	
	♡ K 10 9 8 4 3 2	
	◇ 10 8 3	
	♣ —	

West	**North**	**East**	**South**
Zmudzinski	Piekarek	Balicki	Smirnov
			2◇*
dbl¹	2♡²	2NT	all pass

1. 13-15 balanced or 19+.
2. Pass or correct.

South's seven-card Multi would not be a universal choice. When North used the 'pass or correct' bid of 2♡ East felt he had enough to try 2NT and that contract could not be defeated.

An immediate overcall

After the next player overcalls the opening bid of 2◇ in a major, whether at the two- or three-level, a double by responder should be negative, asking opener to pass if he has that suit or to make a descriptive bid. For example, if the auction starts 2◇-(2♡)-dbl-(pass) opener will pass with hearts, bid 2♠ with a minimum weak two, 3♠ with a maximum, and 2NT if strong and balanced (with decent hearts and 20-22 you may decide to pass the double, of course).

Here is an example from the 2009 Lady Milne Trophy:

E-W vul.

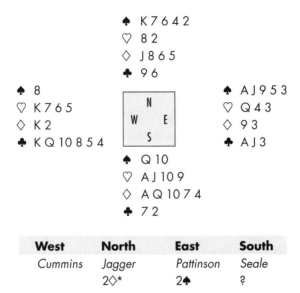

	♠ K 7 6 4 2	
	♡ 8 2	
	◊ J 8 6 5	
	♣ 9 6	

♠ 8		♠ A J 9 5 3
♡ K 7 6 5	**N**	♡ Q 4 3
◊ K 2	**W E**	◊ 9 3
♣ K Q 10 8 5 4	**S**	♣ A J 3

	♠ Q 10	
	♡ A J 10 9	
	◊ A Q 10 7 4	
	♣ 7 2	

West	North	East	South
Cummins	*Jagger*	*Pattinson*	*Seale*
	2◊*	2♠	?

Now South can make a negative double, inviting North to pass with spades.

When the opponents overcall 2♡ it is still possible to stop in 2♠, but when the overcall is 2♠ the negative double commits your side to at least 3♡ (unless partner's suit happens to be spades). After 2◊-(2♠)-dbl opener can bid 3♡ with a minimum weak two in hearts, or, with a maximum, 3♣ or 3◊ as semi-natural game tries.

Here is an example from the 2007 Venice Cup Final in Shanghai:

N-S vul.

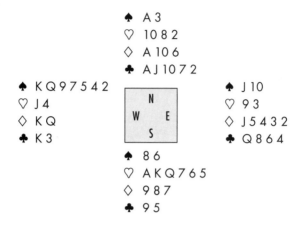

♠ A 3
♡ 10 8 2
◇ A 10 6
♣ A J 10 7 2

♠ K Q 9 7 5 4 2
♡ J 4
◇ K Q
♣ K 3

♠ J 10
♡ 9 3
◇ J 5 4 3 2
♣ Q 8 6 4

♠ 8 6
♡ A K Q 7 6 5
◇ 9 8 7
♣ 9 5

West	North	East	South
Meyers	S-Meuer	Levin	Alberti
		pass	2◇*
2♠	dbl*	pass	3♡
3♠	all pass		

What can we say about South's decision to rebid only 3♡ ? Taking a charitable view we will put it down to inexperience — clearly, since North's double has already committed your side to the three-level, you should jump to 4♡ with such a wonderful suit.

With reasonable support for both majors, responder may be able to make a potentially useful lead-directing bid, as shown in this example from the 2006 McConnell Cup in Verona:

Both vul.

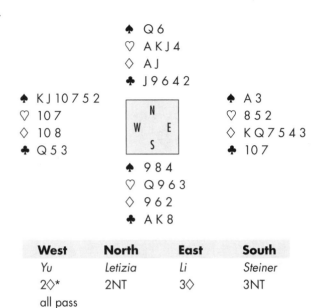

```
                    ♠ Q 6
                    ♡ A K J 4
                    ◇ A J
                    ♣ J 9 6 4 2
♠ K J 10 7 5 2                          ♠ A 3
♡ 10 7              N                   ♡ 8 5 2
◇ 10 8         W        E               ◇ K Q 7 5 4 3
♣ Q 5 3            S                    ♣ 10 7
                    ♠ 9 8 4
                    ♡ Q 9 6 3
                    ◇ 9 6 2
                    ♣ A K 8
```

West	North	East	South
Yu	Letizia	Li	Steiner
2◇*	2NT	3◇	3NT
all pass			

The 3◇ bid took away South's chance to use Stayman, and North-South found themselves comitted to the wrong game on sub-minimum values. East did not find a spade lead, but it did not matter and 3NT finished three down. On accurate defense 4♡ is doomed as well.

After an overcall of 2NT/3♣/3◇, a double is for penalties. A bid of 3♡ is competitive, opener passing with hearts or converting to 3♠. A cuebid of the overcaller's suit is game-forcing. If responder jumps to 4♡ or 4♠, he wants to play there.

Opener's Rebid after Interference

If responder takes no action over an opposing double or overcall, opener will pass at his second turn unless he has a strong balanced hand or an exceptionally distributional weak two-bid.

If opener has 20-22 HCP, he then has two possibilities, one of which is a reopening double for takeout. With a hand that is unsuitable for a takeout double opener can rebid 2NT or a new suit. For example with:

♠ K 7 4 3   ♡ A 8   ◇ A Q   ♣ A Q J 9 8

if the next player overcalls 2◇ with 2♡ then the choice at his next turn is between double and 2NT.

QUIZ

1. You are dealer as West on each of the following hands. Would you open a Multi 2◇?

a) E-W vul.

♠ K Q J 10 9 7 2   ♡ 10 9   ◇ J   ♣ 8 4 2

b) Neither vul.

♠ J 9 8 7 5 3   ♡ K Q 6   ◇ K 2   ♣ 4 2

c) Both vul.

♠ A Q 9 6 5 2   ♡ J 2   ◇ J 8 5   ♣ J 2

d) N-S vul.

♠ A Q 4 3   ♡ A Q 9 2   ◇ A K 10   ♣ K 4

e) Both vul.

♠ K Q J 10 7 4   ♡ 8 4   ◇ A 6 3   ♣ 9 5

f) E-W vul..

♠ Q 3   ♡ A K 9 8 5 2   ◇ 8 7 3 2   ♣ J

g) Neither vul.

♠ 8 7 2   ♡ A K Q 8 7 3   ◇ 8 4 2   ♣ 9

2. Now try your hand at responding, remembering to plan how you intend to develop the auction. Partner (West) has opened 2◇ in each case.

a) Both vul.

♠ J 7   ♡ A 4   ◇ A K 7   ♣ Q 10 8 6 5 3

b) Neither vul.

♠ A K   ♡ J 7 5   ◇ A 8 7 4 3   ♣ Q 6 3

c) N-S vul.

♠ K Q J 7 3 ♡ 10 6 4 ♢ Q 9 6 ♣ J 2

d) Both vul.

♠ A J 8 5 3 ♡ K 9 6 ♢ 9 8 3 2 ♣ 9

e) N-S vul.

♠ A Q J 10 2 ♡ J ♢ 5 4 3 ♣ Q 10 4 3

f) Neither vul.

♠ J 7 ♡ 9 7 6 4 3 ♢ 10 2 ♣ A Q 10 3

g) Neither vul.

♠ 6 5 4 ♡ Q 10 8 4 ♢ — ♣ A Q J 10 3 2

h) N-S vul.

♠ A K J 9 8 7 5 ♡ A ♢ Q 10 9 7 2 ♣ —

i) N-S vul.

♠ 9 8 4 ♡ K 7 5 ♢ J 3 2 ♣ Q 10 9 6

3. Here's a problem where RHO comes into your auction:

E-W vul.

West	North	East	South
	2♢	3♣	?

♠ K 6 ♡ Q 9 6 ♢ A Q 10 9 6 ♣ A 8 7

ANSWERS

1. a) You might open this with 2◇, but unlike a hand we quoted earlier you don't have the sterile 7-2-2-2 distribution, and the right choice is 3♠.

b) Despite the poor quality of your suit, you are worth 2◇. If partner responds 2♡ you will bid 2♠. You will pass a response of 2♠ and over the inquiry of 2NT you should probably treat this as a bad/intermediate hand and bid 3◇.

c) By contrast with the previous example, here your suit is better, but the rest of the hand is quite poor, so you should still treat this as a bad/ intermediate hand.

d) With 22 points you can open 2◇ and then rebid in notrump.

e) You might open this 2◇, but the modern approach is to open 1♠. Exponents of the Acol system that is popular in the UK will tell you they have been doing it for years!

f) This is an automatic 2◇ opening. The quality of the heart suit and the reasonable distribution compensate for the poor location of the other high cards and we would classify this as a good hand.

g) In the 2008 World Bridge Games, every player holding this hand who was playing Multi opened 2◇.

2. a) You could bid conservatively with 2♡, but partner may have a maximum, in which case you should have some play for game. Respond 2NT, intending to stop at the three-level if partner indicates a bad/ intermediate hand by bidding 3♣ (hearts) or 3◇ (spades). If partner shows a good hand by bidding 3♡ (spades) or 3♠ (hearts), you will go on to game. Partner's hand:

$$♠A Q 10 9 4 2 \quad ♡8 7 3 \quad ◇9 5 \quad ♣K 7$$

In the 2009 Senior Camrose both pairs bid to 4♠ after a 2◇ opening.

b) You have exactly the same number of high card points as on the previous hand, so you might think the correct answer is obviously 2NT. However, we consider this to be a much worse hand and would do no more than bid 2♠. The distribution is worse (no potential source of tricks in a side suit) and the high cards are more defensive in nature. In the 2008 World Bridge Games, one player tried 2NT and then went on to 3NT over her partner's rebid of 3◇. Her partner's hand (shown in Problem 1b) was :

♠ J 9 8 7 5 3   ♡ K Q 6   ◇ K 2   ♣ 4 2

As it happens 3NT, while a dreadful contract, could not be defeated as North held the ♣AK and the ♠Q was doubleton! However, that does not mean we condone the bidding.

c) With sound support for both majors it must be right to cramp the auction with a 'pass or correct' jump to 3♡. In the 2008 World Bridge Games partner held:

♠ 9 4   ♡ Q J 8 7 5 3   ◇ 8 7   ♣ A 8 4

The 3♡ contract was three down, but -150 was a bargain against the +660 recorded at the other table.

d) This hand is even better than the preceding one and we would not hesitate to bid 2♠. Partner is unlikely to have spades, but we will be very comfortable in 3♡, or even in 4♡ if our system allows partner to bid that with a maximum.

e) It's virtually certain that partner has hearts, so the right response is 2♡.

f) If partner has a weak hand it is most likely to be in spades. If he happens to have hearts then it is possible that North-South can make a lot of tricks in spades. Bidding 2♡ would not be a mistake, but we would prefer the more aggressive 2♠, just in case. As it happens, on this deal from the 1995 World Championships in Beijing, partner rebid 2NT with

♠ A K 10 3   ♡ A K Q J   ◇ 5 4   ♣ K 9 2

and East transferred to hearts, leading to the cold game.

g) With terrific support for hearts and sound support for spades, you want to contest the auction. Even so, the most practical start is probably 2♠, intending to raise 3♡ to 4♡. Partner's hand in the World Bridge Games 2008 was

♠ K 10 8 7 3 2   ♡ 9 7   ◇ K Q 7 4   ♣ 7

and the wasted diamond values meant that 2♠ was more than high enough.

h) Although it does not come with a written guarantee you should bid 4♠, hoping partner will deliver something useful or that the distribution will be favorable. Partner's hand in fact was:

♠ 3   ♡ K 8 7 5 4 2   ◇ K 6 5   ♣ 9 4 2

and declarer lost two diamonds and a trump.

i) With three-card support for both majors and the vulnerability in your favor you can afford to jump preemptively to 3♡.

3. With some values known to be on your right you need to do more than simply compete with this hand. The way to locate partner's major is to bid 4♣. In the 2008 World Bridge Games, West held:

♠ A 9 3   ♡ K J 8 7 5 3   ◇ 4 3   ♣ 6 5

and 4♡ was easy with the ◇K onside.

CHAPTER 3

ADVANCED IDEAS

THE WEAK-ONLY MULTI

Many partnerships like to adopt a freewheeling style, especially when the position and vulnerability is in their favor. For them, in first and third positions a five-card suit is just as likely as a six-card suit; indeed, hyperaggressive pairs are willing to open at the three-level with a six-card suit, such is the potential gain from preempting the opponents. In less favorable conditions, vulnerable and/or in second position, they tend to be more upright citizens, but might still open with a sound five-card suit. They are certainly not afraid to open with four cards in the other major — on balance the rewards are greater than the risks involved.

In North America, it is quite common to see pairs playing a version of the Multi that does not include a strong option (its practitioners include Meckwell and Kit Woolsey/Fred Stewart). The rationale behind this approach is that responder is not inhibited by the possibility that opener might have a strong hand, especially when responder has a modest hand.

A weak-only option means that responder is completely free to pass the opening bid of 2◇, and some pairs are happy to consider doing this even without diamond length. Here's an example:

♠7 ♡KJ9642 ◇J94 ♣1095

The idea of passing 2◇ with these cards is that a traditional response of 2♡ or 2♠ will usually result in a contract of 2♠ on a 5-1 or 6-1 fit (and possibly doubled). If the bidding dies at 2◇ the hope is that -50 or -100 per trick will turn out reasonably well. If someone doubles 2◇ then responder can retreat to 2♡, which is likely to be the best spot for the partnership.

On hands where responder would usually bid 2♡, aggressive partnerships are alive to the fact that in general terms this is the response that is least likely to put the opposition under pressure. Whilst they have a sound constructive method that can be utilized when required, they appreciate that the main aim of the Multi is to create problems for the opponents. Even a well-prepared pair may well find themselves in difficulties, and those who are not will almost certainly struggle.

Let's look at some specific sequences where a weak-only version is in operation:

West	North	East	South
2◇	pass	2♡	pass
2♠	pass	2NT	

This asks for a feature, indicating that opener's rebid of 2♠ has now opened up the possibility of game.

West	North	East	South
2◇	pass	2♠	pass
?			

2NT   Minimum with hearts
3♣   Maximum with hearts

The advantage of developing the auction this way is that responder may want to play in 3♣ or 3◇ and these sequences make that possible. Playing in this style responder can bid his better major immediately. If opener passes, responder will not be able to introduce his minor, but at least the partnership will be in their best major-suit fit. This approach can also make it difficult for the opponents, as they may not be able to judge the degree of fit that they themselves might have.

After one of these simple pass-or-correct auctions, a bid of 3♣ or 3◇ by responder is to play. Similarly, the sequence:

West	North	East	South
2◇	pass	2♡	pass
2♠	pass	3♡	

says responder wants to play in 3♡. Likewise:

West	North	East	South
2◇	pass	2♠	pass
2NT/3♣	pass	3♠	

says responder wants to play in 3♠.

The 2NT Relay

Playing a weak-only Multi, you still need a way to develop the auction when responder is interested in game or more. This is achieved by using the 2NT relay.

Here is a possible set of replies:

West	North	East	South
2◇	pass	2NT	pass
?			

3♣	Hearts minimum
3◇	Spades minimum
3♡	Spades maximum
3♠	Hearts maximum, five-card suit
3NT	Hearts maximum, six-card suit
4♣	Hearts maximum, four clubs
4◇	Hearts maximum, four diamonds
4♡	Hearts maximum, four spades

If opener shows a minimum hand responder can sign off in three of the major. Otherwise the next step is a relay, asking about trumps. In reply, anything other than the next step by opener shows more than a minimum with six trumps.

When opener has a second suit, he has to decide if it is worth showing if doing so takes the bidding beyond 3NT — the quality of the suit will be all-important.

West	North	East	South
2◇	pass	2NT	pass
3♣	pass	?	

3◇	Asks about heart length
3♡	To play (but did have game interest)
4♣	PKCB for Hearts*
4◇	Unspecified minor-suit slam try
4NT	Blackwood*

We should mention that the acronym PKCB stands for Preemptive Key Card Blackwood — after a weak two-bid (or a three-level opening) a 4♣ bid is used as a keycard ask (after 3♣, 4◇ would be the ask, as 4♣ would be natural). The standard responses are:

1st step	0 keycards
2nd step	1 keycard
3rd step	1 keycard + the trump queen
4th step	2 keycards
5th step	2 keycards + the trump queen

West	North	East	South
2◇	pass	2NT	pass
3♣	pass	3◇	pass
?			

3♡   A five-card suit. Now if responder has slam ambitions he can use 4♣ as PKCB for hearts and 4NT as simple Blackwood

3♠   Six hearts and four spades, after which responder can continue:

4♣	Slam try in hearts
4◇	Slam try in spades
4♡	To play

4♠	To play
4NT	PKCB for hearts
5♣	PKCB for spades

3NT   A six-card heart suit; responder can continue with:

4♣	PKCB for hearts
4♢	General slam try in hearts (bid 4♡ to reject)
4♡	To play
4NT	Regular Blackwood

4♣   Six hearts and four clubs; responder can continue:

4♢	PKCB for clubs
4♡	To play
4♠	PKCB for hearts
4NT	Unspecified slam try in hearts or clubs (bid first rejection)
5♣	To play

4♢   Six hearts and four diamonds. The auction continues now like this:

4♡	To play
4♠	PKCB for diamonds
4NT	PKCB for hearts
5♣	Unspecified slam try in hearts or diamonds (bid first rejection)
5♢	To play

When opener has spades and a minimum the auction continues like this:

West	North	East	South
2♢	pass	2NT	pass
3♢	pass	?	

3♡	Asks about spade length
3♠	To play but did have game interest
4♣	PKCB for spades
4♢	Unspecified minor slam try
4NT	Regular Blackwood

After the 3♡ relay, the continuations are as follows:

3♠ Five-card spade suit. Now if responder has slam
ambitions he can use 4♣ as PKCB for spades and
4NT as simple Blackwood

3NT Six-card spade suit

4♣ Six spades and four clubs. Now:
  4◇ RKCB for clubs
  4♡ Unspecified slam try in spades or clubs (bid
    first rejection)
  4♠ To play
  4NT RKCB for spades
  5♣ To play

4◇ Six spades and four diamonds
  4♡ Unspecified slam try in spades or clubs (bid
    first rejection)
  4♠ To play
  4NT PKCB for diamonds
  5♣ PKCB for spades
  5◇ To play

4♡ Six spades and six hearts

When opener has spades and a maximum the auction looks like this:

West	North	East	South
2◇	pass	2NT	pass
3♡	pass	3♠	pass
?			

3NT Five-card spade suit. Now if responder has slam
ambitions he can use 4♣ as PKCB for spades and
4NT as simple Blackwood.

4♣	Six spades and four clubs	
	4◇	RKCB for clubs
	4♡	Unspecified slam try in spades or clubs (bid first rejection)
	4♠	To play
	4NT	RKCB for spades
	5♣	To play

4◇	Six spades and four diamonds	
	4♡	RKCB diamonds
	4♠	To play
	4NT	RKCB for spades
	5♣	Unspecified slam try in hearts or diamonds (bid first rejection)
	5◇	To play

It is worth emphasizing that when responder has determined opener's suit (and length if he asks for that) an immediate bid of 4♣ is PKCB and as long as 4♣ is available then 4NT is simple Blackwood.

When considering the type of hand that responder might have for 2NT it is possible to include those based on a long, strong minor suit. After the initial response to 2NT, a bid of 4◇ by responder shows a slam try in an unspecified minor. Opener then uses the following step responses:

1st step	No slam interest in either suit
2nd step	Interest in clubs
3rd step	Interest in diamonds
4th step	Interest in clubs and diamonds

For those who like a memory aid you might notice that you use the two highest steps if you like diamonds.

After the step response responder can sign off, make a further try with 4NT or bid a slam. If responder bids 4NT remember that opener still doesn't know responder's suit, so he uses first rejection in light of what he has previously shown; i.e. he makes the lowest bid in the suit in which he is *not* interested in continuing.

This is how it unwinds:

West	North	East	South
2◇	pass	2NT	pass
3♣	pass	4◇	pass
?			

4♡   No slam interest in either suit
     4NT   Still interested (bid first rejection, clubs or
           diamonds)
     5♣   To play
     5◇   To play

4♠   Interest in clubs
     4NT   Still interested (bid first rejection)
     5♣   Slam try in clubs
     5◇   To play

4NT Interest in diamonds
     5♣   To play
     5◇   Slam try in diamonds

5♣   Interest in clubs and diamonds
     5◇   Slam try in diamonds

THE MECKWELL MINI MULTI

The following is an approximation of Jeff Meckstroth and Eric Rodwell's
weak-only version of the Multi. (Meckwell also play their own defense to
Multi, which is described later in Chapter 4.)

Not vulnerable, the point range for the 2◇ opening is 4-9 and the
major suit can be five, six or seven cards in length. A five-card major
should be at least QJ8xx, but any six-card major is allowed and a seven-
card major would be one that was unsuitable for a three-level preempt.
Meckwell tend not to have four cards in the other major and would
probably not open 2◇ with

♠7 ♡QJ954 ◇AQ109 ♣984

Vulnerable, the range widens by a fraction to 4-10 points and should always be a strong five-card suit (such as QJ1098, KQ1097, KQJ87 or AKJ65), a six-card suit, or a seven-card suit unsuitable for the three-level. Meckwell don't open if the suit and hand are too weak.

Here is an example of a Meckwell 2◇ opening bid from the 1986 World Open Pairs in Bal Harbour:

Both vul.

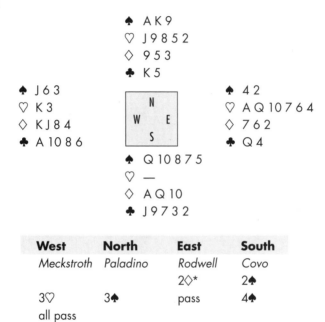

	♠ A K 9	
	♡ J 9 8 5 2	
	◇ 9 5 3	
	♣ K 5	
♠ J 6 3		♠ 4 2
♡ K 3		♡ A Q 10 7 6 4
◇ K J 8 4		◇ 7 6 2
♣ A 10 8 6		♣ Q 4
	♠ Q 10 8 7 5	
	♡ —	
	◇ A Q 10	
	♣ J 9 7 3 2	

West	North	East	South
Meckstroth	*Paladino*	*Rodrigo*	*Covo*
		2◇*	2♠
3♡	3♠	pass	4♠
all pass			

It is worth noticing that West did not make a negative double hoping his partner held spades, but simply competed in what he expected to be his partner's suit. South's raise to 4♠ was dubious, especially playing pairs, and his contract went three down.

The basic responses are standard but they have some specialized sequences:

2NT	Relay		
	3♣	Minimum weak two-bid	
		3◇	GF Relay — opener bids the major he does not have
		3♡	Pass or correct
		3♠	Pass or correct
	3◇	Intermediate with hearts	
	3♡	Intermediate with spades	
	3♠	Maximum with hearts	
	3NT	Maximum with spades	

3♣	Non-forcing, natural
3◇	GF natural
3♡	Pass or correct
3♠	Natural, invitational
3NT	To play
4♣	Transfer to your major
4◇	Bid your major
4♡	Pass or correct
4♠	To play

This pass-or-correct auction is from the 1992 Olympiad in Salsomaggiore:

Neither vul.

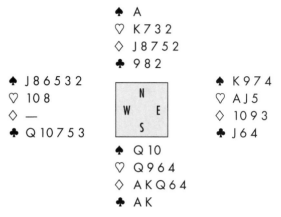

```
                    ♠ A
                    ♡ K 7 3 2
                    ◇ J 8 7 5 2
                    ♣ 9 8 2
  ♠ J 8 6 5 3 2              ♠ K 9 7 4
  ♡ 10 8          N          ♡ A J 5
  ◇ —         W       E      ◇ 10 9 3
  ♣ Q 10 7 5 3    S          ♣ J 6 4
                    ♠ Q 10
                    ♡ Q 9 6 4
                    ◇ A K Q 6 4
                    ♣ A K
```

West	North	East	South
Meckstroth	Salib	Rodwell	T. Sadek
2◇*	pass	3♡*	dbl
3♠	4♡	pass	pass
dbl	pass	4♠	dbl
all pass			

4♡ made at the other table, so 4♠ was a good save. It was even better when North-South misdefended and allowed Meckstroth to make it.

Here is an example of the 4♣ transfer response in action from the 1986 World Open Pairs in Bal Harbour:

Both vul.

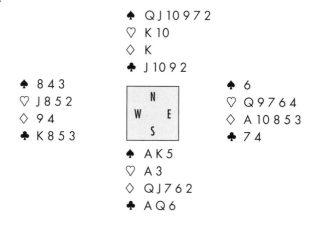

```
            ♠ Q J 10 9 7 2
            ♡ K 10
            ◇ K
            ♣ J 10 9 2
♠ 8 4 3                         ♠ 6
♡ J 8 5 2        N              ♡ Q 9 7 6 4
◇ 9 4        W       E          ◇ A 10 8 5 3
♣ K 8 5 3        S              ♣ 7 4
            ♠ A K 5
            ♡ A 3
            ◇ Q J 7 6 2
            ♣ A Q 6
```

West	North	East	South
Ferraro	Rodwell	Duboin	Meckstroth
	2◇*	pass	4♣*
pass	4♡*	pass	4♠
all pass			

When West led a club, declarer had twelve tricks.

Using 3♣ and 3◇ to Show a Good Hand with a Major Suit

A problem area for pairs who play the Multi arises when responder has a five-card or longer major suit with at least game interest. The key factor is to determine the degree of support that opener has for responder's suit. You can't do this by simply bidding your suit, as that will put you into a pass-or-correct situation. The solution is to use 3♣ and 3◇ to show hearts and spades respectively. These bids show five or more cards in the major, and ask for partner's length in the suit.

It is possible to reply to this inquiry in a very simple way, using a scheme devised by Canada's Colin and Linda Lee:

2◇-3♣
?

3◇	No heart support, maximum with spades
3♡	Heart support, primary spades
3♠	No heart support, minimum with spades
4♡	Primary hearts

2◇-3◇
?

3♡	No spade support, hearts
3♠	Spade support, primary hearts
4♠	Primary spades

A more complex method of responding devised by Kit Woolsey and Steve Robinson also uses step responses:

1st step	0 or 1 cards in responder's major suit
2nd step	2 cards
3rd step	3 or 4 cards

If opener has three or four-card support his bid commits the partnership to game. If opener has less support responder can stop in three of either major if he wishes. Opener is still allowed to bid on with a maximum since responder has indicated game interest, but he must keep in mind there is likely to be only a seven-card fit.

It is possible that responder might actually hit opener's suit. If that happens, the next four steps are used to show that this has happened:

4th step 5- or 6-card support, short in clubs
5th step 5- or 6-card support, short in diamonds
6th step 5- or 6-card support, short in the other major
7th step 5- or 6-card support, no shortage

Here is a sample auction:

West	North	East	South
2◇	pass	3♣*	pass
3NT[1]			

1. 5- or 6-card support for hearts, short in clubs

Once opener shows three- or four-card support, it establishes responder's suit as trumps. After that a bid of 4♣ or 4◇ is a cuebid and the immediate bid above the trump suit is RKCB.

If opener shows less than three-card support, a four-level minor suit by responder is natural, showing at least 5-5. In this way the initial 3♣/3◇ call acts as a transfer bid, giving responder room to show two suits. After responder shows a second suit, opener may offer to play in his own major or in either of responder's suits. Of his other calls, the lower is RKCB for responder's minor and the higher is a slam try in responder's minor.

Here is how this looks:

West	North	East	South
2◇	pass	3♣*	pass
3◇[1]	pass	?	

1. 0 or 1 hearts

3♡	To play	
3♠	To play	
4♣	Natural, at least 5-5	
	4◇	RKCB for clubs
	4♡	Offer to play
	4♠	Offer to play
	4NT	Slam try in clubs
4◇	Natural, at least 5-5	
	4♡	Offer to play
	4♠	Offer to play
	4NT	RKCB for diamonds
	5♣	Slam try in diamonds
	5◇	To play, no slam interest
4♡	To play	
4♠	To play	

West	North	East	South
2◇	pass	3♣*	pass
3♡¹	pass	?	

1. 1 or 2 hearts

3♠		To play
4♣		Natural, at least 5-5
	4◇	RKCB for clubs
	4♡	Offer to play
	4♠	Offer to play
	4NT	Slam try in clubs
4◇		Natural, at least 5-5
	4♡	Offer to play
	4♠	Offer to play
	4NT	RKCB for diamonds
	5♣	Slam try in diamonds
	5◇	To play, no slam interest
4♡		To play
4♠		To play

West	North	East	South
2◇	pass	3♣*	pass
3♠¹	pass	?	

1. 3 or 4 hearts

4♣	Cuebid
4◇	Cuebid
4♡	To play
4♠	RKCB for hearts

West	North	East	South
2◇	pass	3◇*	pass
?			

3♡	0 or 1 spade	
	3♠	To play
	4♣	Natural, at least 5-5
	4◇	Natural, at least 5-5
	4♡	To play
	4♠	To play
3♠	2 spades	
3NT	3 or 4 spades, sets spades as trumps	
4♣	Spades is my suit, club shortage	
4◇	Spades is my suit, diamond shortage	
4♡	Spades is my suit, heart shortage	
4♠	Spades is my suit, no shortage	

And so forth.

CHAPTER 4

DEFENDING AGAINST THE MULTI

The majority of the time the Multi will be based on a weak two-bid in a major suit, even when the 2♢ opening includes a strong option. However, because the suit is unknown the defenders cannot simply defend as they would against a direct bid of 2♡ or 2♠. For this reason, defenses to the Multi generally try to achieve two basic things: tell partner which suit you think opener holds and include a way of showing a balanced hand in the range of 12-15. Here is the defense we favor:

West	North	East	South
2♢	?		

dbl	a) 12-15, balanced *or*
	b) Very strong one-suited hand *or*
	c) 19+, balanced
2♡	Natural
2♠	Natural
2NT	16-18, balanced
3♣	Good hand with a six- or seven-card suit
3♢	Good hand with a six- or seven-card suit
3♡	Good hand with a six- or seven-card suit
3♠	Good hand with a six- or seven-card suit
3NT	To play, usually based on a long running minor
4♣	5+ hearts and 5+ of a minor
4♢	5+ spades and 5+ of a minor
4♡	To play
4♠	To play

Let's look at some examples.

♠ A Q 4	♠ K Q 9	♠ 5
♡ K 8 7	♡ A J 10	♡ A K Q 9 7 5
◇ J 9 5	◇ A K 6	◇ A 10 4
♣ K 10 5 2	♣ Q J 7 4	♣ A J 10

Start with a double over 2◇ with these three hand types: 12-15 balanced, 19+ balanced or a strong one-suiter.

♠ A 3 ♡ K Q 10 9 5 ◇ K 7 4 ♣ J 10 5

Bid 2♡, natural.

♠ A K J 10 5 ♡ 9 3 ◇ A J 6 4 ♣ 10 5

Bid 2♠, natural.

♠ K J 10 5 ♡ A Q 4 ◇ K 9 3 ♣ A 8 5

Bid 2NT, 16-18.

♠ A 10 5	♠ 8	♠ K 4	♠ K Q J 10 8 4
♡ J 5	♡ A 9 4	♡ A K Q 9 6 4 2	♡ A 6
◇ K 4	◇ A K J 10 7 5 2	◇ 9	◇ K Q J 5
♣ A K Q 9 6 4	♣ K 5	♣ A 10 5	♣ 7

All four of these hands qualify for a natural three-level overcall — good hand, good six- or seven-card suit.

♠ A 6 ♡ K 5 ◇ A K Q J 10 5 2 ♣ J 5

Bid 3NT to play — a long running minor and stoppers in both majors.

♠ —	♠ 5
♡ A K J 10 5	♡ K Q J 9 5 2
◇ A 4	◇ A K J 10 6
♣ K Q J 10 6 5	♣ 7

On both hands, bid 4♣, hearts and a minor; now 5♣ by advancer can be pass-or-correct, while 4NT is a general slam try.

```
♠ K Q J 10 6 5      ♠ A K J 10 6
♡ 8                 ♡ 5 2
◇ A K J 10 5        ◇ —
♣ A                 ♣ K Q J 9 5 2
```

On these hands, bid 4◇, spades and a minor; now 5♣ by advancer can be pass-or-correct, while 4NT is a general slam try.

$$♠ A 4 \quad ♡ K Q J 10 9 7 4 \quad ◇ 9 \quad ♣ A J 5$$

Bid 4♡, to play.

$$♠ K Q J 10 8 4 3 \quad ♡ A 6 \quad ◇ K Q 10 \quad ♣ 7$$

Bid 4♠, to play.

This structure is also applicable to fourth-seat bidding except for these sequences:

West	North	East	South
2◇	dbl	2♡	dbl

This double is takeout of hearts (i.e. 3 or 4 cards in spades)

West	North	East	South
2◇	dbl	2♠	dbl

This double is takeout of spades (i.e. 3 or 4 cards in hearts)

The above defensive method is the most popular one in international bridge. One of its advantages is that it can easily be used in conjunction with another well-known convention, Lebensohl. In the Lebensohl convention, a bid of 2NT by advancer after partner's double of 2◇ forces a rebid of 3♣. Then advancer can pass to show a weak hand with clubs or bid a new suit to show a weak hand. An immediate non-jump bid in a suit at the three-level is constructive.

The convention allows you to distinguish between these hand types:

♠ 8 5 2   ♡ 8 4   ♢ 9 6 4   ♣ 10 9 7 4 2

♠ 8 5 2   ♡ 8 4   ♢ K 7 4   ♣ K Q 10 6 3

Clearly it would be unsatisfactory to have to respond 3♣ on both these hands, leaving partner guessing what to do.

Here is an example of one of the most important bids in the defensive canon: the immediate double promising 12-15 balanced (or a stronger hand). The deal comes from the semifinal of the 1996 Olympiad between Denmark and Indonesia:

Neither vul.

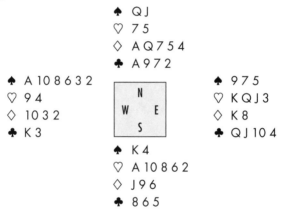

```
              ♠ Q J
              ♡ 7 5
              ♢ A Q 7 5 4
              ♣ A 9 7 2
♠ A 10 8 6 3 2              ♠ 9 7 5
♡ 9 4          N           ♡ K Q J 3
♢ 10 3 2     W   E         ♢ K 8
♣ K 3          S           ♣ Q J 10 4
              ♠ K 4
              ♡ A 10 8 6 2
              ♢ J 9 6
              ♣ 8 6 5
```

Open Room

West	North	East	South
Auken	Lasut	Koch-Palmund	Manoppo
2♠	3♢	3♠	3NT
all pass			

When North overcalled the natural weak two and East made a defensive raise, South felt compelled to venture a speculative 3NT. In our opinion, East might have doubled that for at least +300.

West	North	East	South
Watulingas	*Christiansen*	*Panelewen*	*Blakset*
2◇*	dbl	2♠*	2NT
pass	pass	3♡	pass
3♠	all pass		

Facing what was likely to be a balanced 12-15, South was never going to bid more than 2NT here over East's pass-or-correct intervention. Equally, North was not going to go on unless he had a strong hand. So although East-West landed in a making contract, North-South were never in any danger of getting into trouble.

One question a player must ask is, how good a hand do you need to overcall 2◇ with two of a major? Here is an example from the 2003 Bermuda Bowl in Monte Carlo, where the overcaller's suit was good even though the hand was probably below par. As a result, the overcaller was able to escape unscathed from a potentially dangerous situation.

N-S vul.

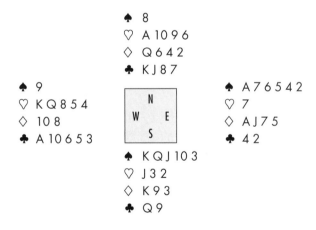

```
              ♠ 8
              ♡ A 10 9 6
              ◇ Q 6 4 2
              ♣ K J 8 7
  ♠ 9                        ♠ A 7 6 5 4 2
  ♡ K Q 8 5 4       N        ♡ 7
  ◇ 10 8        W       E    ◇ A J 7 5
  ♣ A 10 6 5 3      S        ♣ 4 2
              ♠ K Q J 10 3
              ♡ J 3 2
              ◇ K 9 3
              ♣ Q 9
```

West	North	East	South
Antoff	*Bocchi*	*Simpson*	*Duboin*
		2◇*	2♠
dbl	pass	pass	2NT
all pass			

When South overcalled 2♠, West's aggressive double suggested East should pass with spades. When he did so, South removed himself to 2NT, which proved to be a comfortable spot, declarer emerging with nine tricks.

Here is another deal from the same event:

N-S vul.

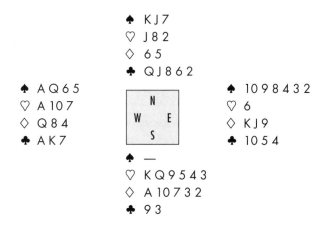

```
                    ♠ K J 7
                    ♡ J 8 2
                    ◇ 6 5
                    ♣ Q J 8 6 2
  ♠ A Q 6 5                          ♠ 10 9 8 4 3 2
  ♡ A 10 7          N                ♡ 6
  ◇ Q 8 4       W       E            ◇ K J 9
  ♣ A K 7          S                 ♣ 10 5 4
                    ♠ —
                    ♡ K Q 9 5 4 3
                    ◇ A 10 7 3 2
                    ♣ 9 3
```

West	North	East	South
Versace	Helness	Lauria	Helgemo
		2◇*	2♡
dbl	pass	2♠	3◇
4♠	all pass		

Once again we see West doubling to suggest that if South happens to have overcalled in East's suit then defending will be a good idea. Notice that not only did Helgemo overcall, he also introduced his second suit.

THE DIXON DEFENSE

As we mentioned in Chapter 1, an April 1976 EBU committee asked Chris Dixon to summarize defenses to the Multi for publication in the May *EBU Quarterly*. The Dixon Defense is still widely used today, although there is more than one version of this popular method.

Over 2◇ the next player uses the following scheme:

dbl	*Either 13-15 balanced or any 20+ hand*
2♡	*Takeout of spades with at least four hearts, non-forcing*
2♠	*Takeout of hearts with at least four spades, non-forcing*
2NT	*16-19 balanced*
3 any	*12-16, good six-card suit*
3NT	*To play*
4♣	*Strong major-minor two-suiter*
4◇	*Strong major two-suiter*
4M	*To play*
4NT	*Strong minor two-suiter*
5m	*To play*

After a double of 2◇, responder can use a Lebensohl response of 2NT. That asks the doubler to rebid 3♣, after which responder can pass with clubs, or bid 3◇ to play, obviously showing a very modest hand in either case.

Dixon in fourth and sixth position

West	North	East	South
2◇	pass	2♡	?

dbl	*Takeout of hearts*
others	*Natural*

West	North	East	South
2◇	pass	2♠	?

dbl	*Takeout of spades*
others	*Natural*

West	North	East	South
2◊	pass	2♡	pass
2♠	?		

dbl   Takeout of spades
others   Natural

Here is an example of a natural overcall after an initial pass from the 2003 Senior Bowl in Monte Carlo:

Both vul.

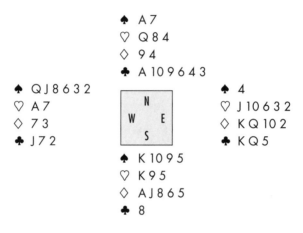

♠ A 7
♡ Q 8 4
◊ 9 4
♣ A 10 9 6 4 3

♠ Q J 8 6 3 2
♡ A 7
◊ 7 3
♣ J 7 2

♠ 4
♡ J 10 6 3 2
◊ K Q 10 2
♣ K Q 5

♠ K 10 9 5
♡ K 9 5
◊ A J 8 6 5
♣ 8

West	North	East	South
Haughie	Schwartz	Walsh	Zeligman
2◊	pass	2♠	pass
pass	3♣	all pass	

Well judged by Zeligman. He knew that in spite of his 11 HCP it would be unwise to bid on. The contract of 3♣ was just made.

Modified Dixon

Most versions of Dixon have one significant disadvantage in that you cannot make a natural overcall of 2♡ or 2♠ and we consider that a huge price to pay.

The following simplified version strikes us as a better option:

dbl	Either 13-15 balanced or any 20+ hand
2♡	Natural
2♠	Natural
2NT	16-19 balanced
3 any	12-16, good six-card suit
3NT	To play
4♣	Strong major-minor two-suiter
4♢	Strong major two-suiter
4M	To play
4NT	Strong minor two-suiter
5m	To play

If the overcaller starts with a double, his partner needs a way to show a modest hand with a minor and this is dealt with in the following set of responses:

West	North	East	South
2♢	dbl	pass	?

2M	Limited, four or more in the major
2NT	Asks partner to bid 3♣ (Lebensohl)
3m	Natural, 8+ points
3M	Natural, forcing to game
3NT	To play

After the sequence:

West	North	East	South
2♢	dbl	pass	2NT
pass	3♣	pass	?

pass	Weak with clubs
3♢	Weak with diamonds
3M	Invitational

After a double and a response of 2M by partner any rebid by the doubler shows 20+, as would a rebid after a pass by partner.

You also need a defense if the bidding starts:

West	North	East	South
2◇	pass	2M	?

This is the standard method:

dbl	Takeout, limited
2♠ (over 2♡)	Natural, limited
2NT	Minors
3♣	Takeout of bid major; strong

You could juggle with these bids, using your preferred combination of double, 3♣ and 3◇ to show weak or strong takeouts, or to include a penalty double. However, we think the best solution is to play the double as unlimited, 2NT as 16-18 balanced and 3♣ as natural.

With a three-suited hand that is short in one major you pass initially and then double for takeout as in these sequences:

West	North	East	South
2◇	pass	2♡	pass
pass	dbl		

West	North	East	South
2◇	pass	2♡	pass
2♠	dbl		

West	North	East	South
2◇	pass	2♠	pass
pass	dbl		

You can also double for takeout in fourth position after:

West	North	East	South
2◇	pass	2M	dbl

A pass followed by 2NT can be used either to show the minors or a hand that would have made a takeout double of the other major. On balance it is probably best to use 2NT in its natural sense, although here is a deal where the first alternative would have worked very well. It comes from the 2007 World Transnational Open Teams in Shanghai:

Neither vul.

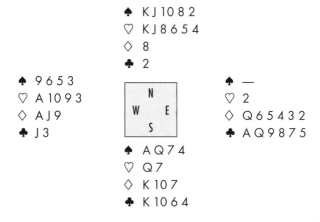

♠ K J 10 8 2
♡ K J 8 6 5 4
♢ 8
♣ 2

♠ 9 6 5 3
♡ A 10 9 3
♢ A J 9
♣ J 3

♠ —
♡ 2
♢ Q 6 5 4 3 2
♣ A Q 9 8 7 5

♠ A Q 7 4
♡ Q 7
♢ K 10 7
♣ K 10 6 4

West	North	East	South
	Senior		*Hecht-Johansen*
pass	2◇*	pass	2♡*
pass	2♠*	pass	4♠
all pass			

When South used the pass-or-correct 2♡, there was a strong possibility that she would have length in spades, so North introduced her 'second' suit and South raised to a game that could not be defeated. However, East missed two opportunities to enter the auction, either by bidding 2NT over 2♠, or by bidding 4NT over 4♠. In either case the easy 5◇ would have been reached — as it was at the other table in this match.

WINTER'S DEFENSE

England international Richard Winter (Mark Horton's old sparring partner) developed another simple defense which is based on the premise that an immediate bid is either intermediate (12-14) or strong (16-18), that a pass followed by a bid is 16-18 or 19-21, and that a double followed by a bid is even stronger. This is how it works:

2nd (and then 6th) position

dbl	Weak notrump
2M	Nonforcing
2NT balanced	15-18 points
3m	Nonforcing
3M	Intermediate
3NT	Long minor, 16-18 to play
4M	To play

A double followed by a second double is for penalties, usually 19+.
A double followed by 3♣ is an artificial forcing takeout with 19+.
A double followed by 2NT shows 22-23.
A double followed by 3NT promises 24-25.

Here is a deal from the 2006 Rosenblum Cup in Verona where the idea of double and then double showing 19+ would have worked very well:

Both vul.

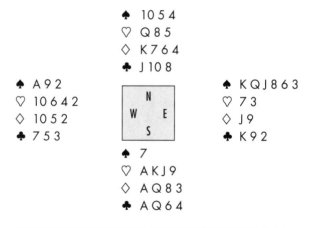

```
                    ♠  10 5 4
                    ♡  Q 8 5
                    ◇  K 7 6 4
                    ♣  J 10 8
  ♠ A 9 2                            ♠ K Q J 8 6 3
  ♡ 10 6 4 2          N             ♡ 7 3
  ◇ 10 5 2        W       E         ◇ J 9
  ♣ 7 5 3            S              ♣ K 9 2
                    ♠  7
                    ♡  A K J 9
                    ◇  A Q 8 3
                    ♣  A Q 6 4
```

West	North	East	South
Kalish	Lindkvist	Podgur	Fredin
	pass	2◇*	dbl
3♡*	pass	3♠	dbl
pass	4◇	pass	5◇
all pass			

South gambled on his partner having a few useful cards and with the ♣K onside he recorded +620. If North had known his partner had 19+ he would surely have elected to pass the second double and collect an easy +800.

Here is an example of an immediate overcall of 2NT from the final of the 2003 Venice Cup in Monte Carlo:

Neither vul.

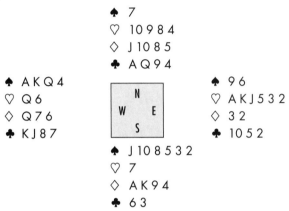

```
              ♠ 7
              ♡ 10 9 8 4
              ◇ J 10 8 5
              ♣ A Q 9 4
  ♠ A K Q 4              ♠ 9 6
  ♡ Q 6          N       ♡ A K J 5 3 2
  ◇ Q 7 6    W     E     ◇ 3 2
  ♣ K J 8 7      S       ♣ 10 5 2
              ♠ J 10 8 5 3 2
              ♡ 7
              ◇ A K 9 4
              ♣ 6 3
```

West	North	East	South
Wang Liping	Seamon-Molson	Zhang	Sokolow
			2◇*
2NT	pass	4◇*	dbl
pass	pass	4♡	all pass

When West showed a strong balanced hand, East drove to game with a Texas-style transfer, but it was very easy for the defenders to score the first five tricks. Lest you think it impossible for East-West to reach the cold 3NT, here is another auction on the same deal, this time featuring the teams contesting the Bermuda Bowl final:

West	North	East	South
Versace	Rodwell	Lauria	Meckstroth
			2◇*
pass	2♠*	3♡	pass
3NT	all pass		

The East-West methods required them to pass with a takeout double of hearts that included four spades, but when East came in over North's nonforcing relay it was easy for West to bid 3NT.

4th seat

dbl	15+ any shape
2NT	15-18 pts bal.
3m	Natural
Jumps	Intermediate/ to play
3NT	Long minor, 16-19, to play

THE ACBL DEFENSES TO MULTI

In North America, the American Contract Bridge League has designated two basic defences to the Multi, and these are available at the table. We have a preference for the more complex Option Two, as it retains 2♡ and 2♠ as natural bids.

Option One

dbl	Takeout of spades. Respond as you would to a double of a weak two-bid, including Lebensohl, if used.
2♡	Takeout of hearts. Respond as to a double of a weak two-bid, including Lebensohl, if used.
Pass, then dbl	Light takeout of the suit doubled.
2♠/3♡	Natural, limited. A response in the other major is a cuebid, jumps natural.
2NT	16-18. Respond as to a 2NT opening.
3m	Natural.
3♠	Strong and natural, 4♡ response is a cuebid.
4m	5+/5+ in the suit bid and a major. Bidding 4◊ over 4♣ asks for the major; bidding 4♡ over 4◊ says pass if you have hearts or correct to spades.

The following doubles are for takeout

West	North	East	South
2◇	pass	2M	dbl

Responses are the same as after a weak two-bid

West	North	East	South
2◇	pass	2M	pass
pass	dbl		

Lebensohl applies if used.

West	North	East	South
2◇	pass	2♡	pass
2♠	dbl		

Lebensohl applies if used.

After

West	North	East	South
2◇	pass	2M	?

dbl	Takeout
2NT	15-18. Respond as to 2NT opening
3m	Natural
3M	Natural
4M	Natural
4m	5+/5+ in that minor and a major. 4◇ over 4♣ asks for the major; 4♡ over 4◇ says pass or correct to spades

After

West	North	East	South
2◊	pass	2♡	dbl
2♠	?		

dbl	Penalty opposite takeout of hearts
3♡	Natural assuming doubler is short in hearts
3♠	Cuebid asking for spade stopper

After

West	North	East	South
2◊	pass	2♡	pass
2♠	pass	pass	dbl

Takeout of spades (same responses as 2♠-pass-pass-dbl).

West	North	East	South
2◊	pass	pass	?

Bid as over a weak 2◊ opening. It's quite rare to see an auction where responder is able to pass 2◊, but as a defender you have to be ready for it. Here is a high-level example from the final of the 2005 Bermuda Bowl between Italy and the USA:

E-W vul.

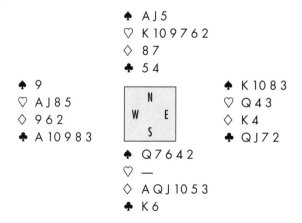

```
                    ♠ A J 5
                    ♡ K 10 9 7 6 2
                    ◊ 8 7
                    ♣ 5 4
   ♠ 9                              ♠ K 10 8 3
   ♡ A J 8 5          N             ♡ Q 4 3
   ◊ 9 6 2        W       E         ◊ K 4
   ♣ A 10 9 8 3       S             ♣ Q J 7 2
                    ♠ Q 7 6 4 2
                    ♡ —
                    ◊ A Q J 10 5 3
                    ♣ K 6
```

West	North	East	South
Nunes	Meckstroth	Fantoni	Rodwell
	2◇	pass	pass
3♣	pass	3NT	all pass

Because Meckwell play a weak-only version of the Multi, South was able to pass the opening bid. That gave West a problem, as his partner might have passed with some strong hands, so he felt he had to balance. East could not be sure how much of his hand his partner had already bid so he naturally took a shot at 3NT, and that drifted two down when South led a diamond.

Option Two
Immediately over 2◇:

dbl	13-15 balanced or any strong hand
2M	Natural. A response in the other major is a cuebid, while a jump in the other major is natural
2NT	16-18. Respond as to a 2NT opening bid
3m	Natural
3M	Strong. A response in the other major is a cuebid.
4m	5+/5+ in suit bid and a major. 4◇ over 4♣ asks for the major; 4♡ over 4◇ says pass or correct to spades

Note: with a takeout double of a major, pass planning to double on the next round; with a strong hand, double directly since 2◇ may be passed.

West	North	East	South
2◇	pass	2/3/4M	?

dbl	Takeout
others	Natural

West	North	East	South
2◇	pass	2M	pass
pass	?		

dbl	Takeout

West	North	East	South
2◇	dbl	2M	pass
pass	?		

dbl   *18+*

West	North	East	South
2◇	pass	2♡	pass
2♠	?		

dbl   *Takeout of spades*

Responses to all these doubles are the same as after a double of a weak two-bid. Lebensohl applies if you normally play it after (2M) – dbl – (pass).

West	North	East	South
2◇	pass	2M	?

2NT   *15-18. Respond as to a 2NT opening*
4m   *5+/5+ that minor and a major. 4◇ over 4♣ asks for major; 4♡ over 4◇ says pass or correct to spades*
3M   *Natural*
4M   *Natural*

West	North	East	South
2◇	pass	2♡	dbl
2♠	?		

dbl   *Penalty*
3♡   *Natural, assuming partner is short in hearts*
3♠   *Asking for a spade stopper*

West	North	East	South
2◇	pass	2♡	pass
2♠	pass	pass	?

dbl   *Takeout of spades (respond as after 2♠-pass-pass-dbl)*

West	North	East	South
2◇	dbl	2M	?

dbl   Balanced with at least invitational values. Does not
      deny a four-card major. If game-forcing, will only
      have a stopper in the major bid

2♠   Natural

2NT   Lebensohl intending to sign off, or game-forcing with
      a minor

3♣   Stayman, game-forcing, continuations as
      after 2NT-3♣

3◇/3♡   Transfers, at least invitational

3♠   Both minors, game forcing

3NT   11-15, stopper in both majors

4m   Strong invitation

4M   Natural

4NT   Blackwood

West	North	East	South
2◇	dbl	2M	2NT
pass	?		

3♣   13-15 balanced

3◇/3♡/3♠   18+, game-forcing

3NT   18-23

West	North	East	South
2◇	dbl	2M	2NT
pass	3♣	pass	?

pass   Weak with clubs

3◇   To play

3♡   Clubs, game-forcing

3♠   Diamonds, game-forcing

3NT   Balanced with stopper only in the major opponent did
      not bid

There is a sequence where the opponents use a pass (or more unusually redouble) to show diamonds:

West	North	East	South
2◇	dbl	pass/rdbl	?

pass	Diamonds!
2M	To play
2NT	Clubs, forces 3♣ with 13-15, then 3◇ shows a forcing club 1-suiter, others natural, with clubs
3♣	Stayman, game-forcing, continuations as after 2NT-3♣
3◇/3♡	Transfers, at least invitational
3♠	Artificial, game-forcing, no diamond stopper
3NT	11-15, stoppers in both majors
4m	Strong invitation.
4M	Natural
4NT	Blackwood

West	North	East	South
2◇	dbl	3 any	?

dbl	Penalties
New suit	One-round force

You can also show a strong hand by cuebidding whatever suit East bids.

If the auction goes like this (which is not allowed by some authorities if a strong option is included):

West	North	East	South
2◇	pass	pass	?

Bid as over a weak 2◇ opening

There are many defenses to the Multi and if you are looking for something esoteric a search on the Internet will reveal a number of possibilities. Including them all is outside the scope of this book, but here are two more that are worthy of mention.

THE MECKWELL DEFENSE TO THE MULTI

It is noteworthy that this is very similar to our preferred defense!

2◇ ?

dbl	13-15 balanced or strong
pass	Followed by double is takeout; pass followed by a new suit is weaker than a direct overcall; pass followed by notrump is for the minors
2♡	Natural
2♠	Natural
2NT	16-18
3♣	Natural
3◇	Natural
3♡	Intermediate good suit
3♠	Intermediate good suit

2◇ pass 2♡ ?

pass	Followed by double is takeout of spades
dbl	Takeout of hearts
2♠	Natural
2NT	15-18
3♣	Natural
3◇	Natural
3♡	Natural (could be played as Michaels)
3♠	Natural, strong one-suiter
3NT	To play
4♣	Natural, strong one-suiter
4◇	Natural, strong one suiter

2◇ pass 2♠ ?

pass	Followed by double is takeout of hearts
2NT	15-18
3NT	To play
3♣	Natural
3◇	Natural
3♡	Natural
3♠	Natural (could be played as Michaels)

2◇   pass   2NT   ?

dbl	Values — if followed by 3NT shows 17-18
pass	Followed by double is takeout
3NT	19-21
others	Natural

2◇   pass   pass   ?

dbl	13-15 balanced or strong
2♡	Natural
2♠	Natural
others	Natural

THE GRANOVETTER DEFENSE

Writing in *Bridge Conventions in Depth* (Master Point Press), Matthew and Pamela Granovetter suggest the following defense:

2◇   ?

pass	When followed by double, takeout
dbl	One major, good hand
2♡	Strong with clubs
2♠	Strong with diamonds
2NT	16-18 balanced
3♣	Natural, limited
3◇	Natural, limited

West	North	East	South
2◇	pass	2M	dbl

Takeout.

And finally…

While we were putting the book together we asked Eric Kokish to comment on these defenses in a couple of Multi sequences:

West	North	East	South
2◇	dbl	pass	?

pass	Promises at least four diamonds
2M	Limited, four or more in the major
2NT	Asks partner to bid 3♣ (Lebensohl)
3♣	Natural, 8+ points
3◇	Natural, 8+ points
3♡	Natural, forcing to game
3♠	Natural, forcing to game
3NT	To play

West	North	East	South
2◇	dbl	pass	2NT
pass	3♣	pass	?

pass	Weak with clubs
3◇	Weak with diamonds
3♡	Invitational
3♠	Invitational

Eric replied:

"Attached is the method I offer victims who don't want to do too much, but using transfer advances wherever possible is the best way to go."

For ambitious readers we have added this magnum opus to the book as an Appendix.

QUIZ

Assume that you are playing our preferred defense, as described at the start of this chapter.

1) E-W vul.

West	North	East	South
2◇	?		

♠ 6 5 3   ♡ A J 4   ◇ A K 10 3   ♣ 10 9 3

2) N-S vul.

West	North	East	South
2◇	pass	3♡*	pass
pass	?		

♠ A 6 5   ♡ K   ◇ K 5 3 2   ♣ K 9 7 6 5

3) E-W vul.

West	North	East	South
2◇	?		

♠ A K 8 7 6 5 2   ♡ K J   ◇ J 3   ♣ 9 8

4) E-W vul.

West	North	East	South
2◇	?		

♠ A J 7 5 3 2   ♡ —   ◇ K Q   ♣ A K 10 9 8

5) Both vul.

West	North	East	South
2◇	pass	2♡	?

♠ K Q 10 9   ♡ 8 4   ◇ A Q 10 4   ♣ A Q 4

6) N-S vul.

West	North	East	South
2◇	pass	2♡	?

♠K965 ♡K74 ◇AK76 ♣AK

7) N-S vul.

West	North	East	South
2◇	?		

♠J10762 ♡A8 ◇AKQ7 ♣A4

8) Neither vul.

West	North	East	South
2◇	?		

♠KQJ1065 ♡J105 ◇K5 ♣AJ

9) Both vul.

West	North	East	South
2◇	pass	2♠	pass
pass	?		

♠K4 ♡A108 ◇1093 ♣A10963

10) Both vul.

West	North	East	South
2◇	pass	2♡	dbl
pass	?		

♠764 ♡Q5 ◇765 ♣K10876

11) Both vul.

West	North	East	South
2◇	?		

♠ A J 9 8 7 3 2   ♡ Q   ◇ Q 9 6 4   ♣ K

12) Both vul.

West	North	East	South
2◇	dbl	2♠	?

♠ K 9 8 2   ♡ J 8 6   ◇ A Q 9 5 2   ♣ 2

13) Neither vul.

West	North	East	South
2◇	?		

♠ A K Q 10 5   ♡ —   ◇ A K 10 9 4   ♣ 10 9 5

14) Both vul.

West	North	East	South
2◇	?		

♠ Q 6   ♡ A K J 4   ◇ A J   ♣ J 9 6 4 2

15) Both vul.

West	North	East	South
2◇	pass	2♡	?

♠ K Q 4   ♡ 6   ◇ A K 9 6   ♣ 10 9 7 6 4

Answers

1) Even though you have a modest hand in terms of high cards, your values are concentrated and you should double, in this case showing 12-15 balanced. In the 2008 World Bridge Games, South held

♠A   ♡KQ32   ◇Q9874   ♣AQ6

and drove all the way to the cold 6◇.

2) Although you had no convenient way of entering the auction on the first round (3♣ would have promised a six-card suit), you can now double to show a three-suited hand, short in one major. This will get you to 3NT when partner has this hand:

♠1082   ♡A92   ◇AJ104   ♣Q103

In the 2008 World Bridge Games, declarer made +660 in 3NT.

3) This is quite a difficult hand to evaluate. You could overcall 3♠, but the distribution is poor and we would be content with 2♠.

4) Your correct action is to jump to 4◇, promising at least 5-5 in spades and a minor. When partner shows interest by bidding 4♡, you mark time by bidding 4♠, but after his further effort of 5◇ you are clearly worth 6♣, after which partner bids 6♠. Partner's hand, from the 2008 World Bridge Games, was

♠K94   ♡AJ5   ◇A1095   ♣654

5) With no heart stopper it would be dubious to bid 2NT. Better to double for takeout, promising three or four spades.

6) Your first thought may be to bid 2NT, but you are too strong for that. Start with a takeout double. If partner bids 2♠ then you can go forward with 2NT.

7) It would not be dreadful to start with 2NT (16-18) but this hand is worth around 19-20 points (you will find a very useful hand

evaluation gadget at http://www.jeffgoldsmith.org/cgi-bin/knr.cgi?hand=
Qxx+AQxx+KQ10+Axx) and the way to get that across is to start
with a double.

8) With such a wonderful suit this hand is worth 3♠. In the 2008 World
Bridge Games, that found partner with

♠A 9 ♡6 ◊A J 6 ♣K 10 7 6 4 3 2

Now one possible sequence to the excellent slam would be:

4♣-4◊; 4♡-4♠; 4NT*-5♠*; 6♠.

9) Is this hand worth a bid? You would like to have a sixth club to bid
3♣, so if you are going to bid then perhaps a takeout double is best. This
is a marginal decision, especially as East is known to have sound values
in support of hearts. We would suggest that a cautious pass is in order.
In the 2008 World Bridge Games, North decided to bid 3♣ and found
partner with:

♠J 10 8 ♡Q 7 6 4 3 ◊6 4 2 ♣Q 5

It cost 500 when 3♣ was doubled.

10) Facing partner's takeout double of hearts you have a modest hand.
The right bid is a Lebensohl 2NT, asking partner to bid 3♣, which you
will pass.

11) Although you have a long suit the rest of your hand is very ordinary
and we think a simple overcall of 2♠ is enough.

12) You have more than enough to bid 3◊, expecting partner to bid on
with one of the strong hands, or with a maximum if he has a balanced
12-15.

13) Another example of a jump to 4◊, promising spades and a minor.

14) This is an awkward hand. You might overcall 2NT (16-18 balanced) but your five-card suit is poor and your spade stopper uncertain. We would prefer to double, treating the hand as 12-15 balanced. In the 2006 World Championships in Verona both bids received approximately equal support. Partner's hand was

♠984 ♡Q963 ◇962 ♣AK8

but nine tricks were the limit in hearts.

15) Paul Soloway's choice in the 1995 World Championships was double, takeout of hearts, promising at least three spades. His partner's hand was

♠AJ32 ♡432 ◇J105 ♣AQJ

(yes, we would have doubled 2◇, showing 12-15 balanced, with that hand).

CHAPTER 5

MUIDERBERG TWO-BIDS

It is fairly well accepted that bridge is a bidder's game — that the side who opens the bidding more often will tend to cause their opponents more problems and in the end score better. Any system that allows you to open weak hands with a fair amount of safety and frequency is one to be given serious consideration.

Since the Multi takes care of weak two-bids in hearts and spades, the opening bids of 2♡ and 2♠ have been freed up for other uses. The optimal method is to use these preemptive bids to describe weak hand types that come up reasonably frequently, but your side should also be able to bid constructively when the occasion arises. In this chapter we describe a popular way of using 2♡ and 2♠: the Muiderberg or Dutch Two-bid. Chess players like to try and surprise their opponents in the opening with a novelty. Muiderberg is the bridge equivalent, a convention that allows a player to open the bidding with minimal values.

The opening schedule is a two-liner:

> 2♡   *5-10 HCP, exactly five hearts and four cards or more in one of the minors*
>
> 2♠   *5-10 HCP, exactly five spades and four cards or more in one of the minors*

♠ 8   ♡ K J 7 4 2   ◊ 8 4 3   ♣ K 10 4 2

Open 2♡.

♠ A Q 6 5 2   ♡ 7   ◊ K J 9 3 2   ♣ 8 5

Open 2♠.

Before we continue, let us show you a deal from the World Bridge Games in Beijng, China in 2008 featuring the teams representing the Netherlands and Mexico.

E-W vul..

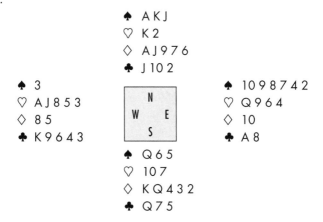

```
                      ♠ A K J
                      ♡ K 2
                      ◇ A J 9 7 6
                      ♣ J 10 2
   ♠ 3                                    ♠ 10 9 8 7 4 2
   ♡ A J 8 5 3          N                 ♡ Q 9 6 4
   ◇ 8 5            W       E             ◇ 10
   ♣ K 9 6 4 3          S                 ♣ A 8
                      ♠ Q 6 5
                      ♡ 10 7
                      ◇ K Q 4 3 2
                      ♣ Q 7 5
```

Open Room

West	North	East	South
	Bertens		Bakkeren
pass	1NT	pass	3NT
all pass			

After this bread-and-butter auction Huub Bertens got a spade lead and ended up with ten tricks. At the table nobody gave much thought to the result and the cards were silently put back in the board. In the other room the outcome on the deal was, to put it mildly, rather different.

Closed Room

West	North	East	South
Westra		Ramondt	
2♡*	dbl	4♡	dbl
all pass			

Even with the trump king offside 4♡ was cold; EW +790. The Netherlands gained 15 IMPs with the double game swing.

This deal is a perfect example of the power of Muiderberg: quick and ruthless bidding to the place you want to be, and maximum pressure on the opponents. Simplicity and effectiveness is what Muiderberg is all about. Hands that are distributed 5442 and 5431 have a much greater frequency than those containing a six-card suit, so hands for Muiderberg Twos are far more frequent than classic weak two-bids. Of course, the vulnerability is a factor. Don't open an ugly 5-count vulnerable against not, but third in hand at favorable vulnerability you may lower your standards drastically.

These methods were developed and used for the first time by two Dutch players: Onno Janssens and Willem Boegem. In the mid-eighties Jan van Cleeff, playing with Janssens, first called the convention 'Muiderberg', which was the name of the village where Janssens lived. Beginning in the 1990s, a number of Dutch bridge players have had great success in the international arena; almost all of them included some type of Muiderberg in their bidding system. Naturally, the vast majority of intermediate players in the Netherlands did the same. Nowadays the majority of the expert bridge world outside North America uses some version of these two-bids. No wonder there is an almost endless list of responses to the opening. We strongly advise you not to over-complicate matters; keep it simple. Remember, Muiderberg is both a preemptive and a constructive device at the same time. There is no need for sophistication.

We offer you two response schedules: the original one by Janssens-Boegem (A) and a second that is rather popular currently in the Netherlands (B).

A. THE ORIGINAL SCHEME

Over a 2♡ opening

2♡   ?

2♠	Natural, invitational (nonforcing)
2NT*	Relay, game forcing or better
3♣	Pass or correct; to play in one of the minors at the three-level
3◇	Invitational relay for a heart game
3♡	Preemptive

3♠	Natural, game forcing
3NT	To play
4m	Splinter
4M	To play

Let's look at examples for each option:

♠ A Q J 7 4 ♡ K 3 ◇ A 7 3 ♣ 10 9 5

Bid 2♠, natural, invitational, non-forcing.

♠ A J 5 ♡ A 10 9 3 ◇ A Q 4 ♣ K Q 7

Bid 2NT, game forcing or better.

♠ J 9 2 ♡ 8 4 ◇ Q 10 5 2 ♣ K J 7 4

Bid 3♣, pass or correct to 3◇.

♠ A 8 ♡ A 10 7 4 ◇ K 8 6 ♣ Q J 9 3

Bid 3◇, invitational relay for a heart game.

♠ 9 5 ♡ J 10 8 7 4 ◇ K J 7 ♣ 10 9 6

Bid 3♡, a preemptive raise.

♠ A K J 10 6 ♡ K 6 ◇ A 4 2 ♣ K Q 3

Bid 3♠, natural, game-forcing.

♠ K Q J 4 ♡ Q 6 ◇ K J 10 ♣ A K 10 7

Bid 3NT to play.

♠ A K Q 9 5 ♡ Q J 8 5 ◇ K 10 6 ♣ 6

Bid 4♣, splinter in clubs.

♠ A J 10 5 ♡ K 10 7 4 3 ◇ 8 ♣ A 7 4

Bid 4◇, splinter in diamonds.

♠75 ♡KJ964 ◇A6 ♣K932

Bid 4♡, to play (most of the time this is going to be preemptive in nature, but as in the example deal above, sometimes all's well that fits well).

♠AQJ109762 ♡— ◇1062 ♣98

Bid 4♠, to play.

After the 2NT relay the bidding continues like this:

West	North	East	South
2♡	pass	2NT	pass
3♣	pass	?	

3♡	Heart fit, slam interest
3♠	Spade stopper, interest in 3NT
4♣	Club fit, slam interest

Those of you with agile minds may like to consider if there is any advantage to reversing the meaning of the 3♡ and 4♣ bids.
    Meanwhile here are examples in each case:

West	North	East	South
2♡	pass	2NT	pass
3♣	pass	3♡	

♠A103 ♡KJ74 ◇KQ6 ♣AQ5

Big heart fit and slam interest.

West	North	East	South
2♡	pass	2NT	pass
3♣	pass	3♠	

♠AKQ5 ♡K6 ◇J93 ♣AQ105

Interest in 3NT, but no diamond stopper. We may end up playing clubs now.

West	North	East	South
2♡	pass	2NT	pass
3♣	pass	4♣	

♠ A Q 6 ♡ K 6 ◇ A 7 4 2 ♣ K Q 8 3

Here we have slam interest in clubs (imagine partner with ace fifth in both hearts and clubs).

When opener shows a diamond suit the situation is similar:

West	North	East	South
2♡	pass	2NT	pass
3◇	pass	?	

3♡	Heart fit, slam interest
3♠	Spade stopper, interest in 3NT
4◇	Diamond fit, slam interest

Here are examples:

West	North	East	South
2♡	pass	2NT	pass
3◇	pass	3♡	

♠ A 10 3 ♡ K J 7 4 ◇ K Q 6 ♣ A Q 5

Slam interest in hearts.

West	North	East	South
2♡	pass	2NT	pass
3◇	pass	3♠	

♠ A K Q 5 ♡ K 6 ◇ A Q 10 5 ♣ J 9 3

No club stopper for notrump this time. Perhaps we shall play in diamonds.

West	North	East	South
2♡	pass	2NT	pass
3◇	pass	4◇	

♠ A Q 6 ♡ K 6 ◇ K Q 8 3 ♣ A 7 4 2

Serious interest in a diamond slam.

Over a 2♠ opening

The responses are similar.

2♠ – ?

2NT*	Relay, game-forcing or better
3♣	Pass or correct; to play in one of the minors at the three-level
3◇	Invitational relay for a spade game
3♡	Natural, invitational (non-forcing)
3♠	Preemptive
3NT	To play
4m	Splinter
4M	To play

Let's look at examples for each option:

♠ A J 5 ♡ A 10 9 3 ◇ A Q 4 ♣ K Q 7

Bid 2NT relay, game forcing or better.

♠ 9 2 ♡ J 8 4 ◇ Q 10 5 2 ♣ K J 7 4

Bid 3♣, pass or correct to 3◇.

♠ A 10 7 4 ♡ A 8 ◇ K J 6 ♣ Q J 9 3

Bid 3◇, invitational relay for a spade game.

♠ K 3 ♡ A Q J 7 4 ◇ A 7 3 ♣ 10 9 5

Bid 3♡, natural, invitational, non-forcing.

♠ J 10 8 7 4 ♡ 9 5 ◇ 10 9 6 ♣ K J 7

Bid 3♠, a preemptive raise.

♠ Q 7 ♡ K Q J 4 ◇ K J 10 ♣ A K 10 7

Bid 3NT to play.

♠ K Q 9 5 ♡ A Q J 8 5 ◇ K 10 6 ♣ 6

Bid 4♣, splinter in clubs.

♠ A J 10 5 ♡ K 10 7 4 3 ◇ 8 ♣ A 7 4

Bid 4◇, splinter in diamonds.

♠ — ♡ A Q J 10 9 7 6 2 ◇ 10 6 2 ♣ 9 8

Bid 4♡, to play.

♠ K J 9 6 4 ♡ 7 5 ◇ K 9 3 2 ♣ A 6

Bid 4♠, to play.

After the 2NT relay the bidding continues like this:

West	North	East	South
2♠	pass	2NT	pass
3♣	pass	?	

3♡	Natural, game-forcing
3♠	Spade fit, slam interest
3NT	For play
4♣	Club fit, slam interest

Here are examples:

West	North	East	South
2♠	pass	2NT	pass
3♣	pass	3♡	

♠ A 6   ♡ A Q J 10 8 6   ◇ J 4   ♣ A J 5

Natural, game-forcing.

West	North	East	South
2♠	pass	2NT	pass
3♣	pass	3♠	

♠ K J 7 4   ♡ A 10 3   ◇ K Q 6   ♣ A Q 5

Slam interest in spades.

West	North	East	South
2♠	pass	2NT	pass
3♣	pass	4♣	

♠ A Q 6   ♡ K 6   ◇ K Q 8 3   ♣ A 7 4 2

Slam interest in clubs.

If opener has diamonds:

West	North	East	South
2♠	pass	2NT	pass
3◇	pass	?	

3♡	*Natural, game-forcing*
3♠	*Spade fit, slam interest*
4◇	*Diamond fit, slam interest*

Here are examples:

West	North	East	South
2♠	pass	2NT	pass
3◇	pass	3♡	

♠ A 6   ♡ A Q J 10 8 6   ◇ J 4   ♣ A J 5

West	North	East	South
2♠	pass	2NT	pass
3◇	pass	3♠	

♠ A J 9 5   ♡ A 6   ◇ K 9 3   ♣ A Q 10 5

West	North	East	South
2♠	pass	2NT	pass
3◇	pass	4◇	

♠ A Q 6   ♡ K 6   ◇ K Q 8 3   ♣ A 7 4 2

Let's try a quick quiz on this:

1. Your partner opens 2♠, Muiderberg. What would you bid with this hand?

♠ 6 5   ♡ Q 10 8 6   ◇ K Q 8 6   ♣ A 5 4

Don't bid 3♣ 'pass or correct'. You don't want to run the risk of ending up in a 4-3 fit at the three-level. Just pass. There is nothing wrong with the 5-2 fit in spades at the two-level.

2. Your partner opens 2♡, Muiderberg. What would you bid with this hand?

♠ 6 5   ♡ Q 10 8 4   ◇ K Q 8 6   ♣ A Q 4

Bid 3◇, invitational to 4♡.

3. Your partner opens 2♡, Muiderberg. What would you bid with this hand?

♠ A 5   ♡ A 10 8 4   ◇ K Q 8 6   ♣ A Q 4

Bid 2NT, game-forcing, and after opener's rebid of 3♣ or 3◇, bid 3♡, showing slam interest for hearts.

B. THE MODERN SCHEME

2♡ – ?

2♠	*Natural, invitational (non-forcing)*
2NT*	*Asks for opener's minor, either for signoff or GF*
3♣**	*Invitational relay (15-17 HCP), no heart fit*
3◇	*Invitational relay for a heart game*
3♡	*Preemptive*
3♠	*Natural, game-forcing*
3NT	*To play*
4m	*Splinter*
4M	*To play*

The 2NT relay

There are obviously two possible rebids for opener.

West	North	East	South
2♡	pass	2NT	pass
3♣	pass	?	

Pass	*Weak with clubs*
3◇	*Natural forcing*
3♡	*Heart fit, slam interest*
3♠	*Spade stopper, interest in notrump*
3NT	*For play*
4♣	*Club fit, slam interest*

Here are some examples of each of these:

♠K74 ♡84 ◇J973 ♣Q1083

Pass.

♠53 ♡A6 ◇AKQ952 ♣KQ4

3◇.

♠A74 ♡KQ73 ◇AJ105 ♣A10

3♡.

♠AQJ5 ♡K10 ◇J74 ♣KQJ6

3♠.

♠AQJ5 ♡K10 ◇KQJ6 ♣J74

3NT.

♠AK64 ♡Q8 ◇A93 ♣KQ94

4♣.

West	North	East	South
2♡	pass	2NT	pass
3◇	pass	?	

Pass   *Weak*
3♡   *Heart fit, slam interest*
3♠   *Stopper, interest in notrump*
3NT   *For play*
4♣   *Natural, forcing*
4◇   *Diamond fit, slam interest*

♠K74 ♡84 ◇J973 ♣Q1083

Pass.

♠ A 7 4 ♡ K Q 7 3 ◇ A 9 ♣ A J 10 5

3♡.

♠ A Q J 5 ♡ K 10 ◇ K Q J 6 ♣ J 7 4

3♠.

♠ A Q J 5 ♡ K 10 ◇ J 7 4 ♣ K Q J 6

3NT.

♠ A 7 3 ♡ 9 ◇ A J 10 ♣ A K Q 10 8 5

4♣.

♠ A K 6 4 ♡ Q 8 ◇ K Q 9 4 ♣ A 9 3

4◇.

The 3♣ relay

These are the continuations after the invitational 3♣ relay, which promises 15-17 points:

West	North	East	South
2♡	pass	3♣	pass
?			

pass   *Minimum with clubs as second suit*
3◇   *Minimum with diamonds as second suit*
3♡   *Maximum with clubs as second suit*
3♠   *Maximum with diamonds as second suit*

After a 2♠ opening

The structure after an opening bid of 2♠ is analogous:

2♠ – ?

2NT*	*Asks for opener's minor for signoff or GF*
3♣**	*Invitational relay (15-17 HCP), no spade fit*
3◇	*Invitational relay for a spade game*
3♡	*Natural, invitational*
3♠	*Preemptive*
3NT	*To play*
4m	*Splinter*
4M	*To play*

These are the continuations after the 2NT relay:

West	North	East	South
2♠	pass	2NT	pass
3♣	pass	?	

pass	*Weak*
3♡	*Natural, game-forcing*
3♠	*Spade fit, slam interest*
4♣	*Club fit, slam interest*

West	North	East	South
2♠	pass	2NT	pass
3◇	pass	?	

pass	*Weak*
3♡	*Natural, game-forcing*
3♠	*Spade fit, slam interest*
4◇	*Diamond fit, slam interest*

These are the continuations after the invitational 3♣ relay:

West	North	East	South
2♠	pass	3♣	pass
?			

pass	Minimum with clubs as second suit
3◇	Minimum with diamonds as second suit
3♡	Maximum with clubs as second suit
3♠	Maximum with diamonds as second suit

Here's a quick quiz on the 'modern' scheme of responses.

1. Your partner opens 2♠, Muiderberg. What would you bid with this hand?

♠ 6 5   ♡ A 6   ◇ K Q 8 6   ♣ A Q 10 5 4

Bid 3♣. You will pass partner's rebid of 3◇, but bid on over the maximum rebids of 3♡ (clubs) or 3♠ (diamonds).

2. Your partner opens 2♡, Muiderberg. What would you bid with this hand?

♠ 6 5   ♡ 5 3   ◇ K J 8 6   ♣ A Q 10 5 4

Bid 2NT and pass opener's rebid in one of the minors.

WHEN THE OPPONENTS ENTER THE BIDDING AFTER A MUIDERBERG TWO-BID

The responses remain unchanged wherever possible.

After a double of 2♡ or 2♠, responder's bids remain unaltered and he also has an extra bid at his disposal, a redouble. Redouble shows values and suggests playing for penalties.

After an overcall in a suit or in notrump, double is penalty. Other bids retain their original meaning, but a raise to the three-level is invitational (instead of preemptive).

How should you defend against a Muiderberg two-bid?

The simplest defense against a Muiderberg two-bid is to treat it as though it were a standard weak two. Thus, a double of a major shows the other major suit and at least opening values. Overcalling in a suit is constructive and a 2NT overcall shows 16-18 HCP with a balanced hand.

Here is a perfect example from the 2006 World Pairs Championship in Verona:

E-W vul..

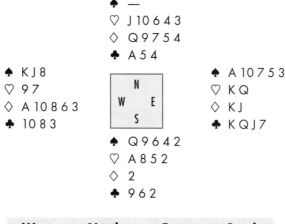

	♠ —	
	♡ J 10 6 4 3	
	◊ Q 9 7 5 4	
	♣ A 5 4	

♠ K J 8		♠ A 10 7 5 3
♡ 9 7		♡ K Q
◊ A 10 8 6 3		◊ K J
♣ 10 8 3		♣ K Q J 7

	♠ Q 9 6 4 2	
	♡ A 8 5 2	
	◊ 2	
	♣ 9 6 2	

West	North	East	South
Auken	*Gromov*	*Christiansen*	*Dubinin*
pass	2♡*	dbl	3♡
pass	4◊	dbl	4♡
4♠	all pass		

After East's double, South made a preemptive raise. With his excellent distribution, North decided to try and confuse the issue and at the same time pave the way to a possible sacrifice by introducing his second suit. Naturally, South preferred to defend against 4♠ (and in any event a heart contract would have been very expensive). However, with careful play, declarer was able to get home.

We will finish this chapter with some examples of Muiderberg in action. This first deal shows how tough it is to contend with Muiderberg, even for a world class pair. The deal was played in the match between Iceland and Poland at the European Champions in Vilamoura, Portugal in 1995.

Neither vul.

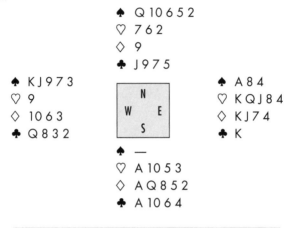

```
                    ♠ Q 10 6 5 2
                    ♡ 7 6 2
                    ◇ 9
                    ♣ J 9 7 5
    ♠ K J 9 7 3                        ♠ A 8 4
    ♡ 9              N                  ♡ K Q J 8 4
    ◇ 10 6 3     W       E             ◇ K J 7 4
    ♣ Q 8 3 2        S                 ♣ K
                    ♠ —
                    ♡ A 10 5 3
                    ◇ A Q 8 5 2
                    ♣ A 10 6 4
```

West	North	East	South
Balicki	Thorbjornsson	Zmudzinski	Baldursson
	2♠*	dbl	2NT*
dbl	3♣	pass	pass
dbl	all pass		

Who could blame Adam Zmudzinski for kicking off with the ♡K? After this lead declarer made nine tricks via a crossruff. Only the lead of the king of trumps would have killed the doubled partscore. Not easy to find, even for Zmudzi.

Take a look at this deal from the 2006 Champions Cup:

N-S vul.

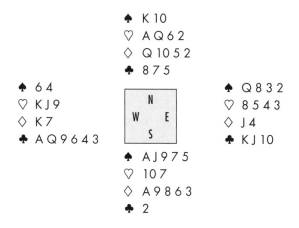

| ♠ K 10 |
| ♡ A Q 6 2 |
| ◇ Q 10 5 2 |
| ♣ 8 7 5 |

♠ 6 4		♠ Q 8 3 2
♡ K J 9		♡ 8 5 4 3
◇ K 7		◇ J 4
♣ A Q 9 6 4 3		♣ K J 10

| ♠ A J 9 7 5 |
| ♡ 10 7 |
| ◇ A 9 8 6 3 |
| ♣ 2 |

West	North	East	South
Kopstad	*Ferraro*	*Kopstad*	*Vivaldi*
		pass	2♠*
3♣	3◇	pass	4♣*
pass	5◇	all pass	

When West overcalled, North was in the fortunate position of being able to bid a forward-going 3◇. With three suits controlled, South decided a cuebid was in order and North jumped to what proved to be an easy game. In the other room the Norwegian South didn't open (although in this era there are many who would) and the final contract was a modest 3◇ – that cost 10 IMPs.

In our methods 3◇ would be invitational for a spade game. So North would pass the 3♣ overcall. If East passes as well, South still might bid 3◇ (etc.). If East raises to 4♣, then North, when the tray comes back to him, has an easy 4◇ (and South will raise to 5◇).

Finally, two Muiderberg deals from the most recent World Championships. A recent article by Pietro Campanile suggested that the idea of opening 2♡ or 2♠ to show a modest major/minor two-suiter was an IMP-losing option. His conclusions are at best questionable, and would certainly have been lost on the Americans after the next deal from the 2009 Senior Bowl in Sao Paulo.

N-S vul.

```
              ♠ —
              ♡ A Q 9 7
              ◇ J 8 5 3
              ♣ A J 7 3 2
♠ A Q J 6 5                      ♠ 9 3 2
♡ K J 10 4        N             ♡ 8 6 2
◇ K           W       E         ◇ 10 7 6
♣ K 10 6          S             ♣ 9 8 5 4
              ♠ K 10 8 7 4
              ♡ 5 3
              ◇ A Q 9 4 2
              ♣ Q
```

West	North	East	South
Passell	*Kowalski*	*Sutherlin*	*Romanski*
		pass	2♠*
pass	2NT*	pass	3◇*
dbl	redbl	pass	pass
3♡	dbl	all pass	

The deal is an illustration of how even a world-class player can go astray in unfamiliar waters. If North had no game interest he could have responded with a pass-or-correct 3♣, so West's entry into a live auction was extremely dubious. While picture-perfect defense could have extracted 1700 from declarer, he was able to escape for a mere 1400 — but it hardly mattered since North-South have only a partscore.

Here is an amusing example from the 2009 Bermuda Bowl in Sao Paulo in the match between Bulgaria and Morocco. It features a Muiderberg opening at both tables!

E-W vul.

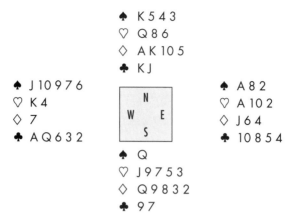

```
                    ♠ K 5 4 3
                    ♡ Q 8 6
                    ◇ A K 10 5
                    ♣ K J
    ♠ J 10 9 7 6              ♠ A 8 2
    ♡ K 4          N          ♡ A 10 2
    ◇ 7         W     E       ◇ J 6 4
    ♣ A Q 6 3 2    S          ♣ 10 8 5 4
                    ♠ Q
                    ♡ J 9 7 5 3
                    ◇ Q 9 8 3 2
                    ♣ 9 7
```

Open Room

West	North	East	South
Aronov	Hayet	Stefanov	Cambournac
			pass
2♠*	2NT	pass	3◇¹
pass	3♡	all pass	

1. Transfer.

When East declined to get involved, North-South settled peacefully in a partscore. On the face of it -140 was nothing special for East-West, but let's move to the other room:

Closed Room

West	North	East	South
Berrada	Karakolev	Rerhaye	Danailov
			2♡*
2♠	4♡	4♠	pass
pass	dbl	all pass	

There is an old adage *'Twice armed is he whose cause is just, but thrice armed is he who gets his blow in first.'* Here it was South who struck first with a Muiderberg two and that produced an auction that rapidly escalated. South led the ♡5 and declarer failed to divine the position in either black suit, finishing with only six tricks, down four, -1100, handing Bulgaria 14 IMPs.

QUIZ

1) N-S vul.

West	North	East	South
?			

♠ 7 6 3 ♡ K Q J 7 4 ◇ Q ♣ Q 6 5 4

2) N-S vul.

West	North	East	South
?			

♠ 10 9 8 6 2 ♡ 4 2 ◇ Q 10 9 7 ♣ K 3

3) Both vul.

West	North	East	South
?			

♠ A Q 10 5 3 ♡ Q 6 2 ◇ 8 7 5 4 ♣ 9

4) Both vul.

West	North	East	South
?			

♠ A 9 ♡ A Q 10 9 2 ◇ 3 ♣ 10 7 6 4 3

5) Neither vul.

West	North	East	South
?			

♠ Q 10 8 7 5 ♡ 3 2 ◇ A Q 8 4 3 ♣ Q

6) Neither vul.

West	North	East	South
2♠	pass	?	

♠ — ♡ A J 8 5 3 ◇ A 6 5 3 ♣ A Q 10 4

7) N-S vul.

West	North	East	South
2♡	pass	?	

♠ K J 8 5 ♡ 3 2 ◇ A 7 4 ♣ K 9 8 6

8) Neither vul.

West	North	East	South
2♡	pass	?	

♠ A Q J 8 6 ♡ 2 ◇ 10 9 5 4 ♣ 9 7 4

9) N-S vul.

West	North	East	South
2♡	pass	?	

♠ K Q 10 8 ♡ Q J 3 ◇ K 8 6 ♣ A J 4

ANSWERS

1) A player using traditional weak twos would probably open your hand 2♡, but has little chance of finding a playable club contract. Open 2♡.

2) Just about the worst hand you could have, and no high cards in your main suit, but the vulnerability is in your favor. Open 2♠.

3) This time your minor suit is woeful, but this is balanced by your superior distribution. Open 2♠.

4) This is an excellent hand, even though you would prefer your black ace to be in clubs. Open 2♡.

5) Two reasonable suits — an automatic 2♠ opening.

6) Despite the fact that you are void in spades there must be a good chance of at least a game, so start with the invitational relay of 3♣ (15-17). Suppose partner rebids 3♠, promising a maximum with diamonds as the second suit? In the 2008 World Bridge Games, East now signed off with 5◇ and found partner with

♠ A Q 10 4 3   ♡ K 9 4   ◇ J 10 9 7 2   ♣ —

Despite the spade void we would suggest the hand is worth a cuebid of 4♣, after which West can bid 4♡ which should ensure that a slam is reached.

7) This is simply a question of reaching the best partscore. Your choices are to pass, trusting that the 5-2 heart fit will be a decent spot, or use the 2NT relay (signoff in partner's minor or game-forcing). On a marginal hand, the possibility of a slightly better fit does not generally compensate for going up a level, so we think a pass is best. In the 2008 World Bridge Games, East tried 2NT and passed the 3◇ reply, making nine tricks when partner produced:

♠ 3 2   ♡ K J 10 9 7   ◇ Q 9 8 5 2   ♣ A

It would have been easy enough to take at least eight tricks in hearts.

The other benefit in passing is that someone may balance — to their disadvantage.

8) This time you want to play in partner's minor, so use the relay of 2NT, planning to pass partner's rebid. In the 2008 World Bridge Games, West's hand was:

♠9 5   ♡A 9 8 7 4   ◇7   ♣A J 10 8 2

and 3♣ made with an overtrick.

9) This hand is a wonderful example of something that we see attempted by countless players — trying to land on a pinhead. It is true that partner may have a very weak hand that offers no play for game, so you might start with one of the relays (3♣/3◇). The trouble is that sometimes even a bare minimum will produce a play for game, so we would bid a direct 4♡.

In the 2008 World Bridge Games, East found partner with a very modest hand:

♠3 2   ♡K 10 9 8 4   ◇4   ♣Q 10 7 6 3

but the ♣K was well-placed and ten tricks rolled home.

CHAPTER 6

2♡ WEAK WITH BOTH MAJORS

We have already outlined the Muiderberg opening bids of 2♡ and 2♠ (major-minor two-suiters) and in this chapter we describe an alternative 2♡ opening bid, one that promises 5-10 HCP with both majors. A significant advantage of this opening bid is that partner will frequently be in a position to raise one of the majors immediately. This hand from the 2009 Spingold final is a typical 2♡ opening using this method:

♠J 10 8 4 2   ♡A J 10 3 2   ◇10   ♣4 3

If you like this option, it still makes sense to play 2♠ as Muiderberg: 5-10 HCP, five spades and a four-card or longer holding in one of the minors.

Before we go any further we want to stress the importance of discipline. It would be unwise to use the 2♡ opening for ultra-light hands. When the opponents enter the bidding on game-going values, they usually don't have much choice. They will either try to penalize you or reach 3NT. For obvious reasons the normal third option, looking for a game in one of the majors, is irrelevant for them. The situation is quite different from interfering over a Multi 2◇ for instance, where the opponents might well explore game possibilities in a major suit. One bonus of a disciplined 2♡ opening bid is that from time to time responder is in good position to double an opponent's 3NT.

Within the 5-10 HCP range, generally speaking, discipline requires a range of 5-8 HCP not vulnerable and a range of 8-10 HCP vulnerable. Of course, distribution is a factor too. Vulnerable, we don't favor opening with 4-4 in the majors even on a 10-count. However, we have no objection to a vulnerable 2♡ on something like:

♠Q J 10 6 5   ♡K J 9 5 3   ◇4 2   ♣7

Quite a few players have been tempted to include the 'weak with both majors' option as part of their strong 2♣ opening. Our view is that this might easily create the wrong kind of uncertainty and we are strongly opposed to this approach. The advantage of the 2♡ opening is that responder immediately knows where he or she wants to be and this allows a preemptive raise in one of the majors. That advantage is lost if the bid is incorporated into the 2♣ opening.

Another disadvantage of including 'weak with majors' in the 2♣ opening is that the bid is much easier to defend against than 2♡ 'weak with majors'. Most of the time, 2♣ will be the weak hand, and with a balanced hand and 13-15 HCP you have a more or less easy double over 2♣. Entering the bidding with such a hand over a 2♡ opening is much more dubious. Partner might have to jump to 3NT on a 10-count, because 2NT is reserved for Lebensohl. Sometimes, however, if you don't enter the bidding with a flat 13-count you might miss game when partner turns out to have 12 or 13 as well.

RESPONSES TO 2♡

As we've seen in the cases of both the Multi 2◇ and Muiderberg Twos, the bidding theorists love to invent complex technology. This applies to the 2♡ opening as well. We like the following effective scheme designed by the Dutch internationals Onno Eskes and Ricco van Prooijen.

> 2♡: 5-10 HCP, normally 5-4 or better in the majors, seldom
> 4-4 (only when third in hand, not vulnerable)

pass	To play, modest hand
2♠	To play, modest hand
2NT	Puppet to 3♣ showing game- or slam-invitational hands or a signoff in clubs
3♣	Game-forcing relay
3◇	To play
3♡	Preemptive; with an extreme hand opener may gamble 4♡
3♠	Preemptive; with an extreme hand opener may gamble 4♠
3NT	To play
4m	Natural and forcing
4M	To play
4NT	Six-ace Blackwood (4 aces and both major-suit kings)

Here are some examples:

$$\spadesuit Q742 \quad \heartsuit 52 \quad \diamondsuit A964 \quad \clubsuit J93$$

Bid 2♠ to play.

♠ 7 4	♠ Q J 3	♠ K 10 4 2
♡ 8	♡ K 10 6 4	♡ A J 6 3
◇ Q 8 4	◇ A J 5	◇ A 5
♣ K Q J 8 7 6 3	♣ A 9 3	♣ A K 6

Bid 2NT, puppet to 3♣, showing game- or slam-invitational hands or a signoff in clubs.

$$\spadesuit KQ74 \quad \heartsuit Q108 \quad \diamondsuit AJ942 \quad \clubsuit A$$

Bid 3♣, game-forcing relay.

$$\spadesuit 9 \quad \heartsuit 74 \quad \diamondsuit KQ108763 \quad \clubsuit K84$$

Bid 3◇ to play.

$$\spadesuit Q4 \quad \heartsuit KJ942 \quad \diamondsuit 75 \quad \clubsuit A642$$

Bid 3♡ preemptive; with an extreme hand opener may gamble 4♡.

$$\spadesuit K10942 \quad \heartsuit J6 \quad \diamondsuit A642 \quad \clubsuit 93$$

Bid 3♠ preemptive; with an extreme hand opener may gamble 4♠.

$$\spadesuit QJ \quad \heartsuit K7 \quad \diamondsuit KQ104 \quad \clubsuit AQJ32$$

Bid 3NT to play.

$$\spadesuit A75 \quad \heartsuit Q2 \quad \diamondsuit 8 \quad \clubsuit AKJ10743$$

Bid 4♣, natural and forcing.

$$\spadesuit K6 \quad \heartsuit KQ842 \quad \diamondsuit 974 \quad \clubsuit A83$$

Bid 4♡ to play.

♠ Q J 9 5   ♡ A 6   ◇ 10 6 3   ♣ A K 9 4

Bid 4♠ to play.

♠ A K 3   ♡ A Q 7 4   ◇ A K J 9 4   ♣ 7

Bid 4NT, six-ace Blackwood.

Six-ace Blackwood (RKCB6)

We advise the use of the following two rules in any RKCB6 situation (and then bid exactly the same as in standard RKCB):

*   *Higher queen: the 'trump queen' is the queen in the higher trump suit (here spades).*
*   *Lower queen: the lower queen is treated as a king in subsequent asks.*

West	North	East	South
2♡	pass	4NT	pass
?			

5♣	1 keycard
5◇	0 or 3 keycards
5♡	2 keycards without the ♠Q
5♠	2 keycards + the ♠Q

More than 3 keycards is impossible within the range of 5-10 HCP.

Looking at our earlier example of a 4NT response:

♠ A K 3   ♡ A Q 7 4   ◇ A K J 9 4   ♣ 7

If partner responds 5♠ you can bid 7♡ with confidence.

The next step over opener's 5♣/5◇ answer asks for the trump queen (the *higher* queen, the ♠Q). Responder can show the trump queen with additional kings, and he treats the ♡Q as a king.

After 5♣

> 5◇ asks for the ♠Q
>
> | | |
> |---|---|
> | 5♡ | No |
> | 5♠ | Yes + no other kings or ♡Q |
> | 6♣ | Yes + ♣K |
> | 6◇ | Yes + ◇K |
> | 6♡ | Yes + ♡Q |

after 5◇

> 5M = signoff; opener bids on with 3 keycards

after 5♡

> 5♠ = signoff

after 5M

> 5NT asks for kings, with the ♡Q treated as a king
>
> | | |
> |---|---|
> | 6♣ | ♣K |
> | 6◇ | ◇K |
> | 6♡ | No ♡Q, no other kings |
> | 6♠ | ♡Q, no other kings |

For example:

♠ K 9 5 3 2	♠ A Q 10 4
♡ K 8 7 5	♡ A 6 3 2
◇ 6 3	◇ A K 5 4
♣ K 2	♣ A

West	North	East	South
2♡	pass	4NT	pass
5♡[1]	pass	5NT[2]	pass
6♣[3]	pass	6♠	all pass

1. 2 keycards, no ♠Q.
2. King-ask.
3. ♣K, so impossible to have the ♡Q as well (otherwise would have opened at the one-level).

Before we look at the continuations after the responses of 2NT and 3♣, here is an interesting deal from the 2006 McConnell Cup in Verona:

Neither vul.

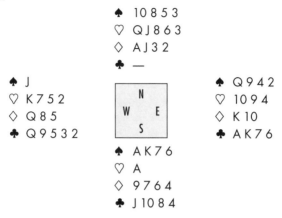

```
              ♠ 10 8 5 3
              ♡ Q J 8 6 3
              ◇ A J 3 2
              ♣ —
  ♠ J                         ♠ Q 9 4 2
  ♡ K 7 5 2                   ♡ 10 9 4
  ◇ Q 8 5                     ◇ K 10
  ♣ Q 9 5 3 2                 ♣ A K 7 6
              ♠ A K 7 6
              ♡ A
              ◇ 9 7 6 4
              ♣ J 10 8 4
```

Open Room

West	North	East	South
Stansby	Sokolow	Rosenberg	Molson
	2♡*	pass	4♠
all pass			

With terrific cards in the majors South rejected any idea of an invitational sequence and jumped to game. It was clear for West to lead a minor, but which one? When she selected a club, declarer was able to bring home ten tricks.

Closed Room

West	North	East	South
Steiner	Meyers	Letizia	Levin
	pass	1NT[1]	pass
pass	2♣[2]	dbl	2♠
all pass			

1. 10-12.
2. Majors.

North's 2♣ bid will be discussed in more detail in a later chapter. With North being a passed hand there was no reason for either player to press for game — just as well, since when West led her trump, nine tricks proved to be the limit.

The 2NT relay

After a response of 2NT the bidding continues like this:

West	North	East	South
2♡	pass	2NT	pass
3♣	pass	?	

pass	Long clubs, to play
3♢	Invitational with 3-3 in the majors
3♡	Invitational with a heart fit
3♠	Invitational with a spade fit
3NT	To play, but convertible (opener is allowed to correct with a six-card suit or with KQJ10x and no entry)
4♣	Slam invitational, agrees hearts
4♢	Slam invitational, agrees spades

The 3♣ relay

This is the structure after the game-forcing response of 3♣:

West	North	East	South
2♡	pass	3♣	pass
?			

3♢	Five hearts + four spades	
	3♡	Sets hearts as trumps
	Other	Cuebid for spades
3♡	Four hearts + five spades	
	3♠	Sets spades as trumps
	Other	Cuebid for hearts

3♠   Four hearts + four spades
        4♣   Sets hearts as trumps
        4◇   Sets spades as trumps

3NT   Five hearts plus five spades
        4♣   Sets hearts as trumps
        4◇   Sets spades as trumps

4♣   Six hearts plus four spades
        4NT   RKCB for hearts
        5♣   RKCB for spades

4◇   Four hearts plus six spades
        4NT   RKCB for hearts
        5♣   RKCB for spades

WHEN THE OPPONENTS INTERFERE

West	North	East	South
2♡	(bid)	?	

dbl   Penalties
others Same as without interference, but with DOPI/ROPI
        after six-ace Blackwood

West	North	East	South
2♡	dbl	?	

redbl   Penalty-oriented
others Same as without interference, but with DOPI/ROPI
        after six-ace Blackwood

DEFENSE AGAINST THE 2♡ OPENING

We suggest the following simple defense to an opening bid of 2♡:

dbl	*13-15 HCP, balanced*
2♠	*Takeout for both minors (preferably 5-5)*
2NT	*16-18 HCP, balanced*
3m	*Natural, very good and long suit*
3M	*Natural, very good and long suit*

THE 2♡ OPENING IN ACTION

Now let's take a look at how the 2♡ bid works out in practice. Sitting West you are dealt this hand:

♠ K ♡ K Q ◇ K Q J 9 7 6 5 2 ♣ J 9

The problem with this type of hand is that it is often not clear where you want to be. If partner has some useful cards, then 3NT, 5◇ or even a slam may be cold. How can we find out more about partner's hand? The answer is not so easy. However, if in first seat, at favorable vulnerability, partner opens with 2♡ 'weak with majors', you immediately know what to do: sign off in a diamond partscore. So:

You	Partner
	2♡
3◇	pass
(to play)	

Sweet and simple. In fact the hand is from a real deal, played between China and Norway in the round robin of the 2009 Yeh Brothers Cup at Australia's Gold Coast:

N-S vul.

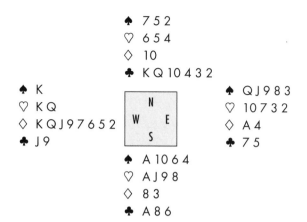

In the open room Jie 'Jack' Zhao and Zhong Fu (China) played in 3◇, just making. In the closed room Geir Helgemo and Tor Helness (Norway) went down one in 4◇.

Here is another deal from the 2009 Yeh Brothers Cup, USA Hampson versus Australia Selected, knockout repechage:

E-W vul.

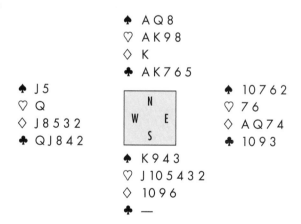

Joe Grue and Curtis Cheek play a big club with asking bids. This enabled the Americans to reach (and make) 6♡ playing North-South. At the other table Ishmael Del'Monte and Robert Fruewirth (Australia) missed the excellent slam, stopping in 4♡.

Playing 2♡ 'weak with majors' would make life easy:

North	South
	2♡
3♣[1]	4♣[2]
5♣[3]	5◇[4]
6♡	pass

1. Game-forcing relay.
2. Six hearts and four spades.
3. RKCB for spades.
4. One keycard.

CHAPTER 7

THE THREE-SUITED 2♡

Another possibility is to use an opening bid of 2♡ to show a limited three-suited hand, a method developed in the UK by Graham Kirby and John Armstrong and taken up enthusiastically by such luminaries as Tony Forrester and Sally Brock.

The basic idea is that with any 4-4-4-1 shape that includes four hearts (and not a singleton queen or king) you open 2♡; the range is 10-15 HCP not vulnerable, 11-15 vulnerable. You can also open 2♡ with 10-15 at any vulnerability with a 0=4=4=5 or 0=4=5=4 distribution (with a five-card spade suit you open 1♠!).

This works well using any methods, but is perhaps most effective when used as part of a strong club system.

These are typical examples of a 2♡ opening:

♠ A 6 4 2	♠ A 7 4 2	♠ —
♡ J 10 5 2	♡ A Q J 5	♡ A J 8 4
◇ A K J 8	◇ 5	◇ K J 10 7 4
♣ 4	♣ K 9 5 3	♣ Q 9 7 3

These are the responses to 2♡:

West	North	East	South
2♡	pass	?	

pass	To play — note that 2♡ is not forcing
2♠	To play opposite four spades and a minimum
2NT	A constructive relay, game invitational or stronger
3♣	To play opposite clubs, opener bids 3◇ if 4=4=4=1
3◇	Natural, invitational opposite a singleton, forcing opposite four trumps
3♡	Natural, invitational, suggests club values if a passed hand

| 3♠ | Natural, invitational opposite a singleton, forcing opposite four trumps |
| 4♡ | Preemptive raise |

♠ 8 5	♠ Q 8 4
♡ J 9 4 2	♡ 10 9 5
◇ A 7 4	◇ Q 7 2
♣ Q 9 8 4	♣ K 9 7 3

Pass.

♠ Q 9 7 3   ♡ 10 5   ◇ A 6 3   ♣ K J 7 4

Bid 2♠ to play opposite four spades and a minimum.

♠ A 9 5	♠ 6 4
♡ K Q 4 2	♡ A K 7 5 3
◇ K 8 7 4	◇ Q
♣ 10 5	♣ A K Q 8 3

Bid 2NT, a constructive relay, game invitational or stronger.

♠ A 9 4   ♡ 10 5   ◇ J 8 5   ♣ K J 10 7 4

Bid 3♣ to play opposite clubs; opener bids 3◇ if 4=4=4=1.

♠ K 8   ♡ 6 2   ◇ K Q 10 9 7 5   ♣ A 7 4

Bid 3◇, natural, invitational opposite a singleton, forcing opposite four trumps.

♠ A 9 5   ♡ K 10 4 2   ◇ K 8 7 4   ♣ 10 5

Bid 3♡, natural and invitational, suggests club values if a passed hand.

♠ K J 10 8 7 5   ♡ A 7   ◇ 10 4   ♣ K 9 3

Bid 3♠, natural, invitational opposite a singleton, forcing opposite four trumps.

♠ 8 5 ♡ K J 10 7 4 2 ◇ A 6 3 ♣ 10 5

Bid 4♡, a preemptive raise.

After a response of 2♠ opener rebids as follows:

West	North	East	South
2♡	pass	2♠	pass
?			

pass	Four spades, minimum
2NT	Singleton or void spade, minimum
3♣	Singleton spade, maximum
3◇	Singleton club, maximum
3♡	Singleton diamond, maximum

♠ A 10 6 2 ♡ K Q 9 4 ◇ Q 5 4 2 ♣ 5

Pass with four spades and a minimum.

♠ 8 ♡ K J 9 5 ◇ A 8 4 2 ♣ Q J 9 3

Bid 2NT, singleton or void spade and a minimum.

♠ 7 ♡ K Q 9 4 ◇ K 10 7 2 ♣ A K 8 4

Bid 3♣, singleton spade, maximum.

♠ A Q 10 3 ♡ A K 8 4 ◇ Q 9 5 2 ♣ 8

Bid 3◇, singleton club, maximum.

♠ K Q 9 3 ♡ K Q 10 4 ◇ 6 ♣ A 9 5 3

Bid 3♡, singleton diamond, maximum.

Here is an example from the match between Great Britain and Germany at the 1991 European Championships:

Neither vul.

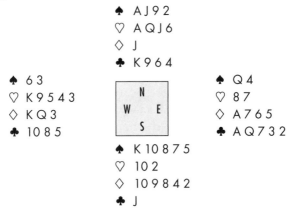

♠ A J 9 2
♡ A Q J 6
◇ J
♣ K 9 6 4

♠ 6 3
♡ K 9 5 4 3
◇ K Q 3
♣ 10 8 5

♠ Q 4
♡ 8 7
◇ A 7 6 5
♣ A Q 7 3 2

♠ K 10 8 7 5
♡ 10 2
◇ 10 9 8 4 2
♣ J

West	North	East	South
Ludewig	Kirby	Bitschene	Armstrong
	2♡*	pass	2♠¹
pass	3♡²	pass	3♠
all pass			

1. To play facing a minimum with spades.
2. Maximum, 4=4=1=4.

There is a case for going on to 4♠ once you discover that partner is maximum and it must have been annoying for John Armstrong to discover that 4♠ was cold.

After the forcing response of 2NT opener rebids like this:

West	North	East	South
2♡	pass	2NT	pass
?			

3♣	Singleton diamond
3◇	Singleton or void spade, 10-poor 12
3♡	Singleton or void spade, good 12-15
3♠	Singleton club, 10-poor 12
3NT	Singleton club, good 12-15

♠Q842 ♡KQ83 ◇6 ♣AJ95

Bid 3♣, singleton diamond.

♠— ♡K1094 ◇A8632 ♣QJ84

Bid 3◇, singleton or void spade, 10-poor 12.

♠9 ♡AJ75 ◇KQ84 ♣A1052

Bid 3♡, singleton or void spade, good 12-15.

♠A853 ♡QJ105 ◇KJ93 ♣5

Bid 3♠, singleton club, 10-poor 12.

♠AK92 ♡QJ86 ◇K832 ♣4

Bid 3NT, singleton club, good 12-15.

After opener has shown a singleton diamond, responder continues as follows:

West	North	East	South
2♡	pass	2NT	pass
3♣	pass	?	

3◇   *Range inquiry, game forcing unless responder passes the response and possibly interested in a slam facing a maximum*

3♡   *Invitational*

3♠   *Invitational*

3NT   *To play*

4♣   *Invitational*

4◇   *Natural & forcing*

4M   *To play*

♠A 9 5 ♡K Q 4 2 ◇K 8 7 4 ♣10 5

Bid 3◇, range inquiry, planning to pass if opener is minimum and rebids
3♡.

♠10 5 ♡K J 9 4 ◇Q 7 5 4 ♣A K 8

Bid 3♡, invitational.

♠K Q 8 3 ♡8 7 ◇Q 9 3 ♣A Q 4 2

Bid 3♠, invitational.

♠K 9 5 ♡Q 8 4 ◇K Q 10 5 ♣A 7 3

Bid 3NT, to play.

♠A 8 ♡K 9 4 ◇10 7 3 ♣K J 10 5 3

Bid 4♣, invitational.

♠K 9 5 ♡A 6 ◇K Q J 10 7 5 ♣A 5

Bid 4◇, natural and forcing.

♠A 8 4 ♡Q J 10 5 ◇A 7 4 ♣K 9 5

Bid 4♡, to play.

♠K J 9 3 ♡K 7 ◇J 7 4 ♣K Q J 3

Bid 4♠, to play.

After the 3◇ range inquiry, opener replies as follows:

West	North	East	South
2♡	pass	2NT	pass
3♣	pass	3◇	pass
?			

3♡	10-11
3♠	12-13
3NT	14-15

After this sequence any bid by responder except 4◇ (see below) sets the
suit and is six-ace Blackwood, with the first step being 0 (with 10-11) or
0-1 (with 12-15).

Here is another example, also taken from the Great Britain v Germany
match at the 1991 European Championships:

Both vul.

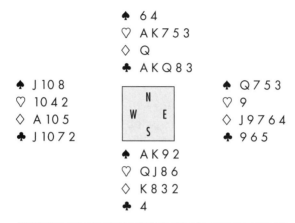

♠ 6 4
♡ A K 7 5 3
◇ Q
♣ A K Q 8 3

♠ J 10 8   ♠ Q 7 5 3
♡ 10 4 2   ♡ 9
◇ A 10 5   ◇ J 9 7 6 4
♣ J 10 7 2   ♣ 9 6 5

♠ A K 9 2
♡ Q J 8 6
◇ K 8 3 2
♣ 4

West	North	East	South
Ludewig	Kirby	Bitschene	Armstrong
		pass	2♡*
pass	2NT*	pass	3NT¹
pass	4♡²	pass	4NT³
pass	6♡	all pass	

1. 4=4=4=1, good 12-15.
2. Sets trumps, six-ace Blackwood.
3. 2 'aces'.

This was just about a laydown.

After a six-ace Blackwood ask, the lowest available of 4NT/5◇ is an
end signal. The next lowest bid available asks for kings. A direct bid
of 4◇ (after a range inquiry) is also an *end signal* — opener bids 4♡ and
responder's next bid sets the final contract. This 4◇ end signal may also
be used when responder employs a three-level bid as six-ace Blackwood
(see the following page for an example).

For example, in this sequence:

West	North	East	South
2♡	pass	2NT	pass
3♣	pass	3◇	pass
3NT	pass	?	

where opener has shown a 4=4=1=4 hand with 14-15, responder would bid 4◇ (end signal) holding:

♠A 9 5   ♡K Q 4 2   ◇K 8 7 4   ♣10 5

and then pass the forced response of 4♡.

If opener shows a shortage in a black suit by rebidding 3◇, 3♡ or 3♠, responder can use a minimum bid of the shortage as an end signal, invitational if opener is 12-15.

Over 3◇ or 3♡, 3♠ is a relay to 3NT if opener is 1=4=4=4 or to 4♣ if 0=4=4=5 or 0=4=5=4, and 3NT is to play. Other minimum suit bids (including 3♡ over 3◇) are six-ace Blackwood, with the first step once again being 0 (with 10-11) or 0-1 (with 12-15). After six-ace Blackwood, if clubs is the shortage, the lowest available of 4♠/4NT/5♣ is an *end signal* and the next lowest bid available asks for kings. If spades is the shortage, 4NT is the end signal and 4♠ asks for kings.

Things are fairly simple if the opponents intervene:

West	North	East	South
2♡	(dbl)	?	

redbl   *Transfer to 2♠ after which responder sets the final contract*

All other bids ignore the double.

West	North	East	South
2♡	(2♠)		

dbl   *Penalties*
3♠   *Asks opener to bid 3NT with a spade stopper, otherwise to bid his lowest four-card suit*

If responder passes, opener will only reopen with short spades and a maximum. All other bids ignore the overcall, as in this example from the 1987 Bermuda Bowl:

Neither vul.

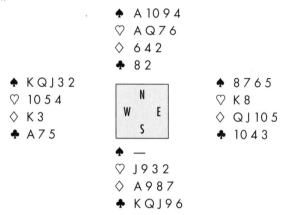

```
                    ♠ A 10 9 4
                    ♡ A Q 7 6
                    ◇ 6 4 2
                    ♣ 8 2
♠ K Q J 3 2                              ♠ 8 7 6 5
♡ 10 5 4            ┌─────────┐          ♡ K 8
◇ K 3              │    N    │          ◇ Q J 10 5
♣ A 7 5            │ W     E │          ♣ 10 4 3
                    │    S    │
                    └─────────┘
                    ♠ —
                    ♡ J 9 3 2
                    ◇ A 9 8 7
                    ♣ K Q J 9 6
```

West	North	East	South
Fallenius	*Armstrong*	*Lindkvist*	*Kirby*
			2♡
2♠	2NT*	3♠	4♣
pass	4♡	all pass	

Here 2NT was the relay and, had East passed, 3♡ would have shown a singleton or void in spades with a good 12-15. When East raised spades, South was able to show his suitability by bidding 4♣. With clubs 3-3, 4♡ could not be defeated, and when Sweden sold out to 3♠ at the other table, Great Britain picked up 8 IMPs on their way to the final.

Over higher intervention up to 4♡, double is to play if opener has four trumps. Otherwise, opener shows range in three steps, after which bids below the end signal are six-ace Blackwood. A cuebid asks opener to bid his lowest four-card suit. A suit bid below a cuebid is to play if opener has four trumps, while a suit bid above a cuebid is natural.

If the opponents overcall at the three-level after the forcing relay, opener's pass shows four poor trumps, or any minimum if the overcall is 3♠ or higher. Double is for penalties while a bid shows a singleton in the intervention suit, after which opener can rebid using the three-step range, where necessary compressing the points so as not to go past 3NT.

QUIZ

1) Both vul.

West	North	East	South
?			

♠ J 8 3 2　♡ K 6 5 4　◇ K　♣ K Q 10 8

2) N-S vul.

West	North	East	South
?			

♠ K Q 7 3　♡ A K J 5　◇ 2　♣ Q 6 5 3

3) E-W vul.

West	North	East	South
2♡	pass	?	

♠ 7　♡ 9 7 6　◇ Q 7 5 3 2　♣ 7 5 4 2

4) Both vul.

West	North	East	South
2♡	pass	2NT	pass
3♣	pass	3◇	pass
3♠	pass	?	

♠ J 6　♡ A Q 10 8　◇ A K Q J 10 8　♣ 8

5) N-S vul.

West	North	East	South
2♡	pass	2♠	pass
?			

♠ A Q 3 2　♡ K 10 3 2　◇ 9　♣ J 7 5 4

6) Neither vul.

West	North	East	South
?			

♠ K 8 6 2 ♡ Q J 8 4 ◇ K 9 4 2 ♣ 8

7) Neither vul.

West	North	East	South
2♡	pass	?	

♠ A 10 8 4 ♡ 10 2 ◇ K Q 10 9 ♣ 8 4 2

8) N-S vul.

West	North	East	South
2♡	pass	?	

♠ A Q 2 ♡ K 6 5 2 ◇ K 9 7 ♣ Q 9 5

9) Neither vul.

West	North	East	South
2♡	pass	2NT	pass
?			

♠ 6 ♡ A K 10 9 ◇ J 9 6 4 ♣ Q 10 8 6

10) Both vul.

West	North	East	South
2♡	pass	?	

♠ K J 2 ♡ 9 8 5 3 ◇ 9 7 3 2 ♣ K 5

11) E-W vul.

West	North	East	South
2♡	2♠	?	

♠ A Q 9 5 ♡ 6 2 ◇ 7 6 5 ♣ K 10 3 2

ANSWERS

1) With a singleton king (or queen) you must not open 2♡. You must either pass or open 1♣ or 1♢.

2) A perfect maximum 2♡ opening.

3) Pass — while it's certain you must have at least an eight-card fit in one of the minors, you have no way to get there and you would be a level higher.

4) After your forcing relay, partner has shown a singleton diamond. In response to your range inquiry, partner promised 12-13. Now 4♡ by you sets hearts as trumps and is six-ace Blackwood. If partner responds 4♠ (0-1) you will have to hope 5♡ is not too high. (Remember that after six-ace Blackwood, the lowest of 4♢/4NT/5♢ is an *end signal* so you would bid 4NT and then sign off in 5♡.)

   If partner bids 4NT (2 keycards) you can either settle for a cautious 5♡ (via the 5♢ end signal), ask for kings with 5♣ (the next lowest bid asks for kings) or gamble that you will not have two spade losers and bid 6♡ (even if you do they have to find the lead).

   If partner bids 5♣ (3 keycards) you can bid 7♡, which will be laydown unless there is a problem in the trump suit.

5) With a bare minimum you should pass.

6) This is not strong enough to open 2♡, and you should pass. Perhaps third in hand at favorable vulnerability you might risk 2♡, but with good defense in three suits we would still be inclined to pass.

7) Respond 2♠, to play opposite four spades and a minimum.

8) Bid 2NT, a constructive relay, game-invitational or stronger.

9) Bid 3♢, singleton or void in spades, 10-poor 12.

10) This is an easy pass of 2♡.

11) If you double here it is for penalties. If you feel cautious then you can pass, since partner will reopen with a singleton spade and a maximum.

CHAPTER 8

THE WEAK 2NT OPENING SHOWING BOTH MINORS

Since it is possible to include strong balanced hands fairly easily in the Multi 2◇ structure, it is possible to assign an interesting new meaning to our 2NT opening. This chapter deals with a 2NT opening bid showing a two-suiter in the minors. Bear in mind that — as implied earlier in the book — our basic schedule for strong balanced hands is the following:

> *20-22 HCP   open 2◇ and rebid 2NT*
> *23-24 HCP   open 2♣ and rebid 2NT*
> *25+ HCP   open 2♣ and rebid 3NT*

But before we go further, let us show you a hand which came up in an internet bridge game, early in 2009. As South you hold:

♠ K 7 4   ♡ K J 6 5 3 2   ◇ Q 7   ♣ 10 5

West is the dealer and you are vulnerable. You have to find a lead after this bidding sequence:

West	North	East	South
pass	pass	4♠	all pass

Of course, you don't have a clue what to lead, as each suit appears to have its advantages or disadvantages. Let us offer a different scenario. Your hand remains unaltered, but the bidding now goes like this:

West	North	East	South
pass	2NT[1]	4♠	all pass

1. Both minors, 5-10 HCP

Leading a minor suit suddenly becomes much more attractive. This was the whole deal:

N-S vul.

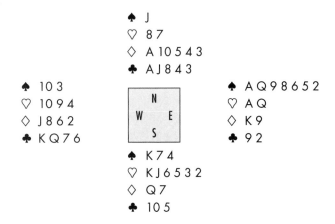

```
                  ♠ J
                  ♡ 8 7
                  ◇ A 10 5 4 3
                  ♣ A J 8 4 3
  ♠ 10 3                            ♠ A Q 9 8 6 5 2
  ♡ 10 9 4          N               ♡ A Q
  ◇ J 8 6 2      W     E            ◇ K 9
  ♣ K Q 7 6         S               ♣ 9 2
                  ♠ K 7 4
                  ♡ K J 6 5 3 2
                  ◇ Q 7
                  ♣ 10 5
```

Faced with the first auction and thus not knowing about the minor two-suiter in North, South led a heart, and declarer was able to assemble ten tricks. A lead in a minor suit (or a passive spade lead) would have left declarer with no chance.

When the deal was finished, North took part of the blame: 'Perhaps I should have bid 4NT, showing minors, when 4♠ came back to me.' That might have worked brilliantly if South had:

♠ 7 4 3   ♡ K 6   ◇ K 7   ♣ K Q 10 7 6 5

East-West would make 4♠ and North-South 5♣.

With the actual layout however, 4NT would prove to be disastrous for North-South. It would have been ridiculous for North to come in at this vulnerability opposite a passed hand. The deal is a glorious advertisement for the opening bid of 2NT, showing minors. It helps you to reach a great contract on minimum values and it also assists you in making the right decisions in defense.

Hereunder we give you two options for the 2NT opening showing minors: a weak version and a weak/strong version.

THE WEAK VERSION OF THE 2NT OPENING

The requirements are at least 5-5 distribution in the minors (with no three-card major suit) and 5-10 HCP. Characteristic hands would be:

♠ 5 ♡ 8 2 ◇ K Q 9 6 3 ♣ Q J 10 4 3

♠ J 5 ♡ — ◇ K Q 9 6 3 2 ♣ K 10 4 3 2

At favorable vulnerability third in hand you could lower your standards. The worst case could be something like this:

♠ 5 ♡ 8 2 ◇ Q 9 7 6 3 ♣ Q 5 4 3 2

The next hand is too strong for 2NT (even vulnerable):

♠ 5 ♡ 8 2 ◇ A Q 9 6 3 ♣ K Q 4 3 2

This is a normal 1◇ opening bid.

Responses to 2NT

This is how responder can continue after a 2NT opening:

West	North	East	South
2NT	pass	?	

pass	No support, both majors
3m	Play, preference
3M	Natural, invitational with a six-card suit
3NT	To play
4m	Natural, invitational
4M	Natural, to play
4NT	Six-ace Blackwood
5m	To play

Responder may choose to jump to game in a minor with a modest hand as a purely preemptive measure when the vulnerability is favorable.

Here are some examples:

$\spadesuit$ A Q 10 3 2 $\heartsuit$ K Q 10 5 $\diamondsuit$ 9 5 $\clubsuit$ 10 4

Pass.

$\spadesuit$ A 9 6 4	$\spadesuit$ K Q 9
$\heartsuit$ K 10 7 3	$\heartsuit$ A 6
$\diamondsuit$ 8 4	$\diamondsuit$ 10 9 5 4
$\clubsuit$ J 9 7	$\clubsuit$ K 9 6 2

Bid 3$\clubsuit$ to play.

$\spadesuit$ Q 9 4 3	$\spadesuit$ K 10 4 2
$\heartsuit$ A Q 7 4	$\heartsuit$ 9 5
$\diamondsuit$ K J 8	$\diamondsuit$ A 9 4 2
$\clubsuit$ 3 2	$\clubsuit$ J 7 3

Bid 3$\diamondsuit$ to play.

$\spadesuit$ 8 4 2 $\heartsuit$ A K J 10 7 4 $\diamondsuit$ Q 5 $\clubsuit$ K 4

Bid 3$\heartsuit$, invitational.

$\spadesuit$ K Q 10 5 $\heartsuit$ A K 10 4 $\diamondsuit$ K 5 $\clubsuit$ A 7 3

Bid 3NT to play.

$\spadesuit$ Q 9 5 3 $\heartsuit$ A 7 4 $\diamondsuit$ K 7 $\clubsuit$ A J 7 3

Bid 4$\clubsuit$, invitational.

$\spadesuit$ A Q J 10 8 4 3 $\heartsuit$ 8 $\diamondsuit$ A 7 $\clubsuit$ K 9 4

Bid 4$\spadesuit$ to play.

$\spadesuit$ A 3 $\heartsuit$ A K 4 2 $\diamondsuit$ K Q 9 $\clubsuit$ A Q 7 5

Bid 4NT, six-ace Blackwood.

```
♠ K 9 5 3        ♠ 6
♡ A 7 4          ♡ 10 7 4
◇ K 7            ◇ J 9 5 3
♣ A Q 7 3        ♣ K J 10 7 4
```

Bid 5♣ to play.

```
♠ A 10 5         ♠ 10 5 3 2
♡ J 10 7         ♡ 6
◇ A Q 5 2        ◇ Q J 9 6 4
♣ A Q 4          ♣ K 5 4
```

Bid 5◇ to play.

We have already encountered six-ace Blackwood in double fit situations. This time the keycards are the four aces and the minor-suit kings. In Chapter 6 we recommended using the following two rules in any RKCB6 situation:

* *Higher queen: trump queen is the queen in the higher trump suit (here diamonds).*

* *Lower queen: lower queen (here the ♣Q) is treated as a king in subsequent asks.*

West	North	East	South
2NT	pass	4NT	pass
?			

5♣	1 keycard
5◇	0-3 keycards
5♡	2 keycards and no ◇Q
5♠	2 keycards + ◇Q

Looking at our earlier example of 4NT:

♠A 3   ♡A K 4 2   ◇K Q 9   ♣A Q 7 5

If partner responds 5♡ (2 keycards) you can bid 7♣ with confidence (or 7NT at matchpoints).

Over opener's 5♣/◇ answer, 5♡ asks for the trump queen (the *higher* queen). Responder can show the trump queen with additional kings, and he treats the ♣Q as a king.

When the opponents interfere

West	North	East	South
2NT	(bid)	?	

dbl   Penalties
others   Same as without interference, but dopi/ropi after six-
ace Blackwood

THE WEAK/STRONG VERSION OF THE 2NT OPENING

The distributional requirements remain unchanged. The range, however, differs: it is either a) 5-10 HCP or b) 18+ HCP. Please note that all bids described hereunder are to be treated as 'invitational', 'to play' or 'game-forcing' opposite the weak version (a). When opener has the strong version (b), he usually makes another bid.

Responder replies like this:

West	North	East	South
2NT	pass	?	

3♣   To play, preference*
3◇   To play, preference**
3M   Natural, invitational with a six-card suit
3NT   To play
4m   Invitational
4M   Natural, to play
4NT   Six-ace Blackwood
5m   To play

After the response of 3♣ the bidding continues like this:

West	North	East	South
2NT	pass	3♣	pass
?			

pass Weak version
All other bids show the strong version, and opener describes his hand as follows:

3◇	*Absolute minimum (although strong version)*
3♡	*2=1=5=5*
3♠	*1=2=5=5*
4♣	*1=1=5=6*
4◇	*1=1=6=5*
4♡	*2=0=5=6 or 2=0=6=5*
4♠	*0=2=5=6 or 0=2=6=5*

After the response of 3◇ the bidding continues this way:

West	North	East	South
2NT	pass	3◇	pass
?			

pass Weak version
All other bids show the strong version, and opener describes his hand as follows:

3♡	*2=1=5=5*
3♠	*1=2=5=5*
3NT	*Absolute minimum*
4♣	*1=1=5=6*
4◇	*1=1=6=5*
4♡	*2=0=5=6 or 2=0=6=5*
4♠	*0=2=5=6 or 0=2=6=5*

Actions by responder

Lets take a look at a few specific examples:

$$♠ J 10 6 4 3 \quad ♡ Q 7 2 \quad ◇ Q 5 \quad ♣ A 9 2$$

After 2NT, responder should simply give preference with 3♣ (but bid to game when partner shows the strong version).

$$♠ A Q J 9 8 4 \quad ♡ 7 2 \quad ◇ K 5 \quad ♣ A 9 2$$

Bid 3♠, game-invitational.

$$♠ A Q J 10 9 8 4 \quad ♡ A 7 2 \quad ◇ K 5 \quad ♣ 9$$

Bid 4♠.

$$♠ A 10 8 4 3 \quad ♡ K 3 \quad ◇ K Q 5 3 \quad ♣ A 9$$

Bid 4◇, invitational.

$$♠ K J 10 8 4 \quad ♡ A 9 5 \quad ◇ K 8 7 3 2 \quad ♣ —$$

Bid 5◇.

$$♠ A K 8 5 4 \quad ♡ A 5 \quad ◇ K Q 7 3 \quad ♣ K 5$$

Bid 4NT, six-ace Blackwood and after:

> *5◇ (0 keycards*) bid pass*
> *5♣ (1 keycard*) bid 6◇*
> *5♡ (2 keycards without ◇Q) bid 7◇*

$$♠ A K 8 5 4 \quad ♡ A 5 \quad ◇ K 7 3 \quad ♣ A K 2$$

Bid 4NT, six-ace Blackwood and after:

> *5◇ (0 keycards*) bid pass*
> *5♣ (1 keycard*) bid 5♡, asking for minor queens. Then:*

after 5♠ (no ◇Q), bid 6♣
after 5NT (◇Q), bid 6♣
after 6◇ (both minor queens), bid 7♣/7◇

* *Theoretically these responses show 1/4 and 0/3 keycards in the usual way. However, in view of all the points you own yourself, it is safe to assume that this time opener does not have the strong version.*

Here is an example of the sort of result the 2NT opening can achieve. It comes from the 2007 final of the Venice Cup in Shanghai, on a deal that we have already featured on page 40.

N-S vul.

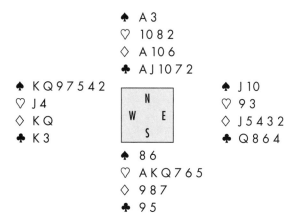

```
                    ♠ A 3
                    ♡ 10 8 2
                    ◇ A 10 6
                    ♣ A J 10 7 2
♠ K Q 9 7 5 4 2                      ♠ J 10
♡ J 4              N                 ♡ 9 3
◇ K Q         W        E             ◇ J 5 4 3 2
♣ K 3              S                 ♣ Q 8 6 4
                    ♠ 8 6
                    ♡ A K Q 7 6 5
                    ◇ 9 8 7
                    ♣ 9 5
```

Open Room

West	North	East	South
von Arnim	Stansby	Auken	Rosenberg
		2NT*	pass
3◇	all pass		

The opening 2NT promised 5-5 in the minors, 4-9 points, and when South was unwilling to balance the Germans had stolen the pot. A slight misdefense saw declarer emerge with seven tricks, -100.

Another — spectacular — example comes from the Open European Championships, San Remo 2009, in a match between Zaleski and White House Juniors:

Neither vul.

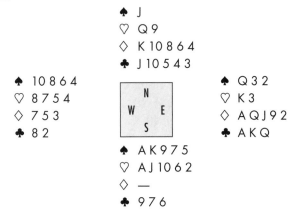

♠ J
♥ Q 9
♦ K 10 8 6 4
♣ J 10 5 4 3

♠ 10 8 6 4
♥ 8 7 5 4
♦ 7 5 3
♣ 8 2

♠ Q 3 2
♥ K 3
♦ A Q J 9 2
♣ A K Q

♠ A K 9 7 5
♥ A J 10 6 2
♦ —
♣ 9 7 6

West	North	East	South
Faigenbaum	*Verbeek*	*Zaleski*	*Molenaar*
pass	2NT*	dbl	3♣
pass	pass	dbl	pass
3♡	pass	3NT	dbl
all pass			

Declarer only made his obvious tricks in the minors: five down, −1400.

QUIZ

1) N-S vul.

West	North	East	South
?			

♠ 5 ♡ Q ◇ Q 7 5 4 3 2 ♣ K Q 10 7 2

2) N-S vul.

West	North	East	South
2NT	3◇¹	?	

1. Strong takeout with better spades than hearts.

♠ J 6 4 ♡ A J 9 ◇ K 9 8 6 ♣ J 6 3

3) N-S vul.

West	North	East	South
2NT	dbl	?	

♠ A 10 9 5 ♡ K 6 4 ◇ 6 4 3 ♣ J 10 8

4) N-S vul.

West	North	East	South
2NT	pass	?	

♠ K Q 7 3 2 ♡ A 10 3 ◇ Q 9 6 5 ♣ J

5) N-S vul.

West	North	East	South
2NT	pass	?	

♠ Q 10 9 ♡ A Q J 5 4 3 ◇ 9 2 ♣ A 2

ANSWERS

1) Open 2NT, 5-10.

2) Bid 5◊, which is sure to be a good save against a major-suit game by North-South.

3) Bid as you would without the double — show preference with 3♣.

4) This is just about worth an invitational 4◊.

5) You might risk 3♡, invitational, with a six-card suit, but we feel the soundest option is to bid 3♣.

CHAPTER 9

THE MULTI LANDY DEFENSE AGAINST AN OPPONENT'S 1NT OPENING

The 'multi' concept — using one bid to show more than one type of hand — is powerful and efficient. If 'multi' bids cost something in terms of obfuscation, making it harder to compete vigorously, the same is true for both sides. It is perhaps not surprising, then, that the idea has been used for more than just the opening two-bid structure.

The opening bid of 1NT is so effective that a whole host of methods have been developed to allow the defenders to compete over it, principally on hands that are unbalanced with some high-card strength. These methods all involve the use of some artificial bids that cannot then be used in a natural sense, but that loss is heavily outweighed by the ability to show many other hand types and the opportunity to enter the auction more frequently.

One of the simplest ways to compete over a 1NT opening is to use a 2♣ overcall to show both majors. This method is called Landy, after the late American expert Alvin Landy, who devised it. Once the Multi 2◇ and related two-suited opening bids gained popularity in Europe, more and more players added similar ideas to the Landy convention over 1NT, thus creating a complete and effective method against the opponent's opening bid of 1NT. Eventually the convention became known as Multi Landy. In North America the same idea was adopted and further developed by Kit Woolsey, and therefore is often referred to as 'Woolsey'.

Nowadays, numerous experts have incorporated Multi Landy into their system, and many variations exist. The specific structure recommended here owes much to the ideas of Maarten Schollaardt, a Dutch international player, who wrote a fine article in *Bridge Magazine IMP* on this subject.

The advantage of Multi Landy is that a great variety of hands can be shown over the opponent's 1NT, thereby achieving the main objective of enabling the overcaller's side to contest the partscore. This is the basic method:

(1NT) - ?

dbl	*Over a weak notrump: penalties*
	Over a strong notrump: a four-card major with a
	longer minor
2♣	*Both majors (usually 5-4 distribution or better)*
2◊	*A six-card major or a good hand with a long minor*
2♡	*Five hearts and a four-card or longer minor*
2♠	*Five spades and a four-card or longer minor*
2NT	*Both minors or a strong two-suiter*
3 any	*Natural, preemptive*
4♣	*Clubs and hearts, very strong*
4◊	*Diamonds and hearts, very strong*
4M	*To play*

These overcalls can be made in second or fourth position. Let's take a closer look at each bid.

(1NT) - dbl

In the old days, a double of 1NT was for penalties, showing the upper HCP range of the opening bid. However, it is rare to pick up a hand powerful enough to double a strong notrump for penalties. Many players prefer the double to have a conventional meaning: a four-card major with a longer minor; that way they can sometimes take the initiative at an early stage in the bidding.

Here is an example where such a conventional double would have worked brilliantly. The deal is from the 2009 Spingold KO Teams in Washington, DC, Round of 16:

Neither vul.

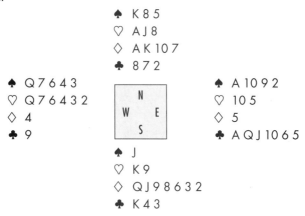

♠ K 8 5
♡ A J 8
◇ A K 10 7
♣ 8 7 2

♠ Q 7 6 4 3
♡ Q 7 6 4 3 2
◇ 4
♣ 9

♠ A 10 9 2
♡ 10 5
◇ 5
♣ A Q J 10 6 5

♠ J
♡ K 9
◇ Q J 9 8 6 3 2
♣ K 4 3

Open room

West	North	East	South
Rubin	*Nickell*	*Ekeblad*	*Katz*
pass	1NT	3♣	3NT
all pass			

East led the ♣A and continued the suit. Declarer ended up with eleven tricks when the defenders gave the show away in hearts, but the contract was always making. However, notice that East was never able to give a good picture of his hand. The East hand perfectly qualifies for a Multi Landy double, showing a major-minor two-suiter. What would West do if he knew about a sure 5-4 fit in one of the majors? It is likely that he would compete at the four-level and bid 4♡ — pass or correct. The result could be spectacular since 4♠ can be made if declarer scoops the ♠J and guesses that South has the ♣K. And when East-West find their spade fit the defense against 5◇ (the contract at the other table) is also much more obvious. East kicks off with the ♠A and is then likely to find the logical continuation of the ♣A and another club.

A double of a weak notrump remains the same: penalty. In the balancing chair the situation does not change, but of course responder can always convert a double of a strong notrump to penalties, as in the next example.

In the quarterfinals of a US Team Trials match, South, at unfavorable vulnerability, was looking at:

♠ K J 7 3   ♡ 10 8   ◊ 9 3   ♣ A K 7 5 3

West opened 1NT (15-17), which was passed round to South. Having no obvious bid in his methods, South passed as well. This was the full deal:

N-S vul.

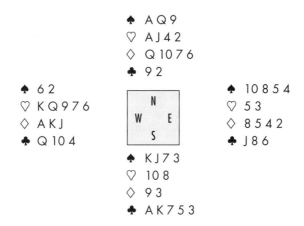

                ♠ A Q 9
                ♡ A J 4 2
                ◊ Q 10 7 6
                ♣ 9 2

♠ 6 2   ♠ 10 8 5 4
♡ K Q 9 7 6   ♡ 5 3
◊ A K J   ◊ 8 5 4 2
♣ Q 10 4   ♣ J 8 6

                ♠ K J 7 3
                ♡ 10 8
                ◊ 9 3
                ♣ A K 7 5 3

A missed opportunity for North-South since they could hurt East-West seriously with a penalty double or could even make a game their way. If North-South had been playing Multi Landy, South could have doubled, showing a four-card major and a longer minor. It would have been easy for North to convert that into penalties by passing.

After a strong notrump (and we would include 14-16), a double shows a four-card major and a long minor. There is no specific number of HCPs required, but at unfavorable vulnerability the South hand shown above can be considered as a minimum. We don't say you shouldn't consider bidding without the ♠J, but replace the ♠K with a small card and bidding becomes unattractive, to say the least. With this understanding, partner can leave the double in with a suitable hand.

Responding to the double

West	North	East	South
1NT	dbl	pass	?

pass   *Happy to defend 1NT doubled (uncommon, since overcaller is usually distributional)*

2♣   *To play in a minor; pass or correct; over a 2◇ rebid, responder may continue 2♡, pass or correct in overcaller's major*

2◇   *Asks partner to bid his major*

2M   *Natural, to play*

2NT   *Artificial, general game try, at least 4-4 in the majors. Overcaller rebids his minor with a minimum, or his major or 3NT with a maximum.*

We suggest that responder should be 4-4 (or better) in the majors to bid 2◇, so that with a suitable hand the doubler can jump to the three-level as an invitation to game. However, doubler should keep in mind that responder might be very weak, so he should have a pretty good hand, for example:

♠ 5   ♡ A K 10 8   ◇ 10 5   ♣ A K Q 9 5 2

With this hand you can afford to jump to 3♡.

If they redouble

West	North	East	South
1NT	dbl	redbl	?

Woolsey recommends agreeing that pass here is to play, and otherwise ignoring the redouble (i.e. bids mean the same as if East had passed). There are other things one can do of course, but it is not a bad philosophy to ignore enemy doubles and redoubles in conventional situations and have bids mean what they would have meant had the enemy passed — much easier on the memory.

(1NT) - 2♣

The 2♣ overcall shows both majors, usually a 4-5 or a 5-4 distribution.
With a 4-6 or 6-4 one has the choice between 2♣, showing both majors,
or 2◇, showing a six-card major. With a good six-card suit and a bad
four-card suit, the hand can be treated as a one-suiter; with a bad six-card
suit and a good four-card suit, the hand should be treated as a two-suiter.
At favorable vulnerability, a 4-4 distribution is allowed, especially in the
balancing seat. The 2♣ overcall may also include 5-5 distributions. The
really strong hands should be treated differently, as we will show later
in this chapter.

The million dollar question, of course, is how strong the 2♣ overcall
should be. The answer is not so easy: it all depends on vulnerability
and distribution. A serious partnership must develop an understanding
of which hands are or are not suitable to compete with. To give you an
idea:

♠ Q J 10 4   ♡ K J 9 2   ◇ K 6 5   ♣ 4 2

At favorable vulnerability, overcall 2♣. At any other vulnerability, pass.

♠ Q J 10 4 3   ♡ K J 9 2   ◇ K 6 5   ♣ 4

At unfavorable vulnerability, pass. At any other vulnerability, bid 2♣.

♠ Q J 10 4 3   ♡ K Q 9 2   ◇ A 6 5   ♣ 4

At any vulnerability, bid 2♣.

In the 2006 World Championships in Verona a 2♣ overcall was made on
all these hands:

Not vul. vs. vul.

♠ Q J 10 6   ♡ K 10 9 7 6 3   ◇ A   ♣ 5 3

Both vul.

♠ J 8 7 6 4   ♡ Q J 8 5 3   ◇ A   ♣ K J

Not vul. vs. vul.

♠ Q J 10 4   ♡ A 10 9 7 6   ◇ J   ♣ J 8 4

Vul. vs. not vul.

♠ Q 6 5 4 3   ♡ Q 9 8 4 3   ◇ A K   ♣ 3

Continuing the auction when partner overcalls 2♣

West	North	East	South
1NT	2♣	pass	?

pass	Long clubs, no interest in the majors
2◇	Equal length in both majors, partner gives preference
2M	Preference
2NT	Forcing; usually invitational to game in one of the majors. See below
3M	Natural, preemptive

After:

West	North	East	South
1NT	2♣	pass	2NT
pass	?		

overcaller can rebid as follows:

3♣	Better hearts, not minimum
3◇	Better spades, not minimum
3♡	Longer hearts (or 4-4), minimum
3♠	Longer spades, minimum
3NT	5-5 or better, maximum

West	North	East	South
1NT	2♣	dbl	?

redbl	Long diamonds
others	Unchanged

(1NT) - 2◇

The 2◇ overcall is typically Multi style: it guarantees a six-card suit in either hearts or spades. When considering the requirements of suit quality and point count we consider that, as before, the vulnerability is all-important. In addition, the overcall can be based on a good hand with a minor.

Let's look at an example of a competitive auction at the top level. It comes from one of the great deals of all time. We go back to the year 2003: the battle for the Bermuda Bowl between the United States and Italy in Monte Carlo was nearing its end. On this deal, Multi Landy proved to be instrumental in taking and holding the initiative in the bidding:

Neither vul.

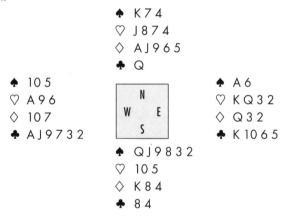

	♠ K 7 4	
	♡ J 8 7 4	
	◇ A J 9 6 5	
	♣ Q	

♠ 10 5		♠ A 6
♡ A 9 6		♡ K Q 3 2
◇ 10 7		◇ Q 3 2
♣ A J 9 7 3 2		♣ K 10 6 5

	♠ Q J 9 8 3 2	
	♡ 10 5	
	◇ K 8 4	
	♣ 8 4	

West	North	East	South
Hamman	*Lauria*	*Soloway*	*Versace*
pass	pass	1NT[1]	2◇*
3NT	4♡[2]	dbl	4♠
pass	pass	dbl	all pass

1. 14-16 HCP.
2. Pass or correct.

East-West can take four tricks against 4♠. However, West led a spade and after Paul Soloway won the ace, he played back another trump. With the aid of a good guess and a fortuitous diamond position, Versace now made his doubled contract with an overtrick. In the other room, the Italians were allowed to play in 3NT and made ten tricks. The double game swing gained the Azzuri 15 IMPs, moving them three ahead of USA. Still, the Americans survived, and when the smoke cleared they had won the match and the world title by the smallest of margins: 1 IMP. But that's another story.

What are the requirements for a 2◊ overcall?

Usually the bid promises a six-card major just like a 2◊ opening bid. This implies a flexible approach within the three ranges: a bad weak two, an intermediate weak two or a good weak two. Again, the vulnerability plays an important role. Vulnerable against not, it would be unwise to overcall with the South hand Versace held in our last example. Even at the actual vulnerability his overcall was still a bare minimum. The 2◊ overcall can also be based on a good hand with a minor, but with a poor hand and long diamonds responder is still allowed to pass.

Let's have a look at some continuations:

West	North	East	South
(1NT)	2◊	(pass)	2♡*
(pass)	?		

pass	Six- (seven-) card heart suit (three ranges)
2♠	Six- (seven-) card spade suit (three ranges)
3 any	Very good hand, six (seven) cards in the bid suit

Here is a straightforward example from the 2006 Women's World Pairs Championship in Verona:

Neither vul.

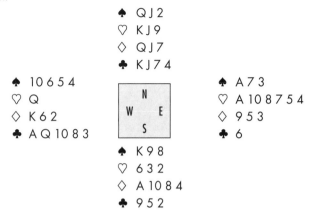

```
              ♠ Q J 2
              ♡ K J 9
              ◇ Q J 7
              ♣ K J 7 4

♠ 10 6 5 4          N          ♠ A 7 3
♡ Q             W       E      ♡ A 10 8 7 5 4
◇ K 6 2             S          ◇ 9 5 3
♣ A Q 10 8 3                   ♣ 6

              ♠ K 9 8
              ♡ 6 3 2
              ◇ A 10 8 4
              ♣ 9 5 2
```

West	North	East	South
Auken	Campagnano	Molson	Baroni
	1NT	2◇*	pass
2♡*	all pass		

The bidding made it clear that declarer should not hazard the club finesse and she finished one down.

Here are some examples of bad, intermediate and very good 2◇ overcalls:

♠ J 10 8 5 4 2	♡ Q 4	◇ A 6 3	♣ 8 2	Bad
♠ K J 10 8 5 4	♡ Q 4	◇ A 6 3	♣ 8 2	Intermediate
♠ A K J 10 8 4	♡ K 4	◇ A Q 3	♣ 8 2	Very good

West	North	East	South
(1NT)	2◇	(pass)	2♠*
(pass)	?		

pass	Six- (seven-) card spade suit
2NT	Very good hand, six (seven) cards in hearts
3m	Very good hand, six (seven) cards in the bid minor
3♡	Six (seven) cards in hearts, minimum
3♠	Very good hand, six (seven) cards in spades
4♡	Six (seven) cards in hearts, maximum

For instance, with:

♠ 7 5   ♡ A 5   ◊ A 3   ♣ A K J 10 8 5 4

RHO opens 1NT, you overcall 2◊ and over any relay by partner you bid 3♣.

West	North	East	South
(1NT)	2◊	(pass)	2NT*
(pass)	?		

3♣   *Bad/intermediate weak two in hearts*
       (now 3◊ is "Last Train")
3◊   *Bad/intermediate weak two in spades*
       (now 3♡ is "Last Train")
3♡   *Good weak two in spades*
3♠   *Good weak two in hearts*
3NT *Very good hand, six (seven) cards in a minor*

(1NT) - 2♡/2♠

These overcalls are very similar to the Muiderberg opening bids described in Chapter 5. Here are some examples and a simple response structure. Suppose you have:

    ♠ 7 4   ♡ K J 10 9 4   ◊ A Q 5 4 2   ♣ 7
or

    ♠ A J 9 8 7   ♡ 3   ◊ K Q 10 6   ♣ K 4 3

and your RHO opens 1NT.

With both hands you would like to take a bid, even vulnerable against not. The Muiderberg method allows you to introduce your five-card major at the two-level, even when your opponents have already opened the bidding with a strong notrump. So just overcall 2♡ and 2♠ respectively on these hands. This guarantees exactly a five-card suit in the bid major and a four-card or longer minor suit. In principle this method is not designed to play in the minor suit, but to substantially reduce the risk of being doubled for penalties. With shortness in the bid major, responder to the Muiderberg bid knows that there might be a much better fit in the minor.

Responses:

West	North	East	South
(1NT)	2♡	(pass)	?

pass	To play
2♠	Natural, to play
2NT	Asks for minor, forward-going
3♣	Looking for the minor, pass or correct
3◇	Game-invitational in hearts
3♡	Preemptive

West	North	East	South
(1NT)	2♠	(pass)	?

pass	To play
2NT	Asks for minor, forward-going
3♣	Looking for the minor, pass or correct
3◇	Game-invitational in spades
3♡	Natural, invitational in hearts
3♠	Preemptive

(1NT) – 2NT

The 2NT overcall usually shows a two-suiter in the minors. A 5-5 distribution (or better) is advisable since the overcaller commits the partnership to at least the three-level. However, in exceptional cases, 5-4 hands are permitted. It would be a pity not to be allowed to bid over 1NT with a hand like this:

♠6 ♡AQ3 ◇KJ1094 ♣KJ98

But there is more. Take, for instance, this hand:

♠KQJ752 ♡AK9876 ◇3 ♣—

Obviously you don't need much for game, even if the opponents have opened with a strong notrump. The overcall of 2♣ (showing both majors) does not give partner the whole picture and you therefore might miss game. You even run the risk that, with long clubs, partner will pass. The solution is to overcall 2NT instead. The bid includes very strong two-suited hands in almost any two suits. Responder will assume a minor two-suiter until further notice.

Responses:

West	North	East	South
(1NT)	2NT	(pass)	?

3♣	Preference
3◇	Preference
3♡	Preference for clubs, invitational
3♠	Preference for diamonds, invitational
3NT	To play over a weak notrump
4m	Preemptive

This is one way the bidding might continue after the 3♣ response:

West	North	East	South
(1NT)	2NT	(pass)	3♣
pass	?		

pass	Minor two-suiter
3◇	Very strong two-suiter, hearts and diamonds
3♡	Very strong major two-suiter (longer hearts or equal length)
3♠	Very strong major two-suiter (longer spades)
3NT	Very strong minor two-suiter
4♣	Very strong two-suiter clubs and a major
4◇	Very strong two-suiter diamonds and a major

After the 3◇ response:

West	North	East	South
(1NT)	2NT	(pass)	3◇
(pass)	?		

pass   Minor two-suiter
3NT   Very strong minor two-suiter
others Unchanged

Here is an example that shows the 2NT overcall in a good light. It comes from the 2006 Rosenblum Cup in Verona:

N-S vul.

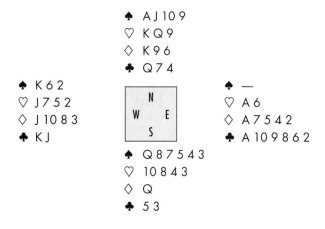

```
                    ♠ A J 10 9
                    ♡ K Q 9
                    ◇ K 9 6
                    ♣ Q 7 4
  ♠ K 6 2                          ♠ —
  ♡ J 7 5 2          N            ♡ A 6
  ◇ J 10 8 3     W       E        ◇ A 7 5 4 2
  ♣ K J              S            ♣ A 10 9 8 6 2
                    ♠ Q 8 7 5 4 3
                    ♡ 10 8 4 3
                    ◇ Q
                    ♣ 5 3
```

West	North	East	South
Hamman	Moss	Soloway	Forrester
pass	1NT	2NT*	pass
4◇	pass	5◇	all pass

With four diamonds and two useful club honors, Bob Hamman was not afraid to raise to 4◇, and with his exceptional distribution and first-round control in every suit, Paul Soloway went on to a game that he made in comfort. At the other table, East had to overcall 3♣, and played there.

Of course there will always be hands with which you would like to make an overcall but which don't seem to fit in with your methods. Take this one, for instance:

♠ K J 10 x x   ♡ A x x   ◇ A K x   ♣ A x

The hand doesn't meet any requirements of the modern version of Multi Landy. Still there is a solution: start with a double. For the time being partner will think that you have some four-card major/longer minor type of hand. After his likely 2♣ response, you correct to 2♠, showing a very strong hand with a five-card spade suit.

QUIZ

1) Neither vul.

West	North	East	South
1NT[1]	?		

1. 15-17.

        ♠J9763 ♡Q1074 ◇K5 ♣A7

2) N-S vul.

West	North	East	South
pass	pass	1NT[1]	?

1. 15-17.

        ♠743 ♡KJ32 ◇KQJ82 ♣J

3) E-W vul.

West	North	East	South
1NT[1]	?		

1. 15-17.

        ♠K3 ♡AQ876542 ◇— ♣A96

4) Neither vul.

West	North	East	South
pass	pass	pass	1NT[1]
?			

1. 15-17.

        ♠109432 ♡AK965 ◇Q2 ♣10

5) E-W vul.

West	North	East	South
pass	pass	1NT¹	?

1. 15-17.

♠ K Q 8 4 2 ♡ J 9 7 6 4 ◇ 9 6 ♣ 9

6) Neither vul.

West	North	East	South
pass	1NT¹	?	

1. 12-14.

♠ A K J 4 ♡ Q 4 2 ◇ 7 3 ♣ A 8 6 5

7) E-W vul.

West	North	East	South
1NT¹	?		

1. 15-17.

♠ A K 10 6 5 2 ♡ 10 6 ◇ 8 6 4 ♣ 10 7

8) N-S vul.

West	North	East	South
1NT¹	2♣	pass	?

1. 15-17.

♠ 4 2 ♡ J 10 6 ◇ K 10 7 6 4 ♣ 9 8 3

9) Neither vul.

West	North	East	South
pass	1NT[1]	?	

1. 15-17.

♠ J 5　♡ A 5　♢ K Q J 9 8 5 3　♣ 7 6

10) Neither vul.

West	North	East	South
pass	1NT[1]	?	

1. 15-17.

♠ 3　♡ A K Q 8 5　♢ 8 6 3　♣ A 8 4 3

11) N-S vul.

West	North	East	South
1NT[1]	?		

1. 15-17.

♠ 9 6 4　♡ K Q J 10 6 5　♢ J　♣ K 8 3

12) Neither vul.

West	North	East	South
pass	1NT[1]	?	

1. 14-16.

♠ A 10 5 3 2　♡ Q 5　♢ 10　♣ J 10 9 6 5

13) Both vul.

West	North	East	South
pass	1NT	2◇	pass
2♠	pass	?	

♠ A 6 5 ♡ A Q J 8 5 2 ◇ K 7 ♣ 9 7

14) N-S vul.

West	North	East	South
		pass	1NT[1]
2◇	pass	?	

1. 15-17.

♠ A 5 2 ♡ 5 4 ◇ K 7 3 ♣ J 10 8 4 2

ANSWERS

1) You would prefer more of your high cards to be in your long suits, but you can still bid 2♣, at least 5-4 in the majors.

2) A double here promises a four-card major with a longer minor. It is just about worth the risk, but keep in mind you are vulnerable and facing a passed hand. In the 2008 World Bridge Games, partner held

♠ 10 9 8 6 5 2   ♡ 9 6   ♢ 4   ♣ K 6 3 2

so 2♠ was a playable spot (and responder could bid 2♠ to play).

3) This is a regulation 4♡ overcall. Partner's hand is

♠ J 8 4 2   ♡ J   ♢ J 10 8 7 4 2   ♣ K 3

and ten tricks cannot be prevented.

4) Despite being a passed hand, you clearly want to compete, which you can do by bidding 2♣, both majors. Partner has

♠ J   ♡ 10 7 4 3   ♢ 8 6 5   ♣ A 8 5 4 3

so you either make a partscore in hearts or easily defeat 3NT.

5) This is a marginal overcall of 2♣, but you are 5-5 and it is generally a good idea to try to disturb 1NT.

6) It would by no means be wrong to pass here, but at the 2008 World Bridge Games, Eric Rodwell was happy to double and with Jeff Meckstroth turning up with

♠ 10 8   ♡ A J 9 3   ♢ Q J 6 4   ♣ 9 7 4

his side collected +300.

7) A bit thin on high cards, but you have an excellent suit, so you can bid 2◊, promising a six-card major. Now partner, holding

♠9 8 7　♡K Q J 5　◊Q 9 7 2　♣A 6

can use the relay of 2NT to discover you have a bad/intermediate weak two in spades (you will reply 3◊) and then sign off in 3♠, which should just make. Trumps were 2-2 when the deal occurred in the 2008 World Bridge Games.

8) No need for any heroics here; give simple preference by responding 2♡.

9) A perfect hand for an overcall of 3◊.

10) You have an excellent hand, and should bid 2♡, promising at least five hearts and a four-card or longer minor.

11) A good suit entitles you to overcall 2◊, even at this vulnerability.

12) You have a very modest hand and are facing a passed partner. Even so, an overcall of 2♠ is attractive as it takes away a lot of their bidding space. At the 2008 World Bridge Games it caused North-South to miss a very reasonable slam.

13) You should bid 2NT promising a very good hand with six (or seven) cards in hearts. Partner's hand at the 2008 World Bridge Games was

♠9 7　♡9 6 4 3　◊J 9 6　♣A J 10 2

and 4♡ was an excellent contract.

14) Respond 2♡ in Multi style, expecting partner to pass with hearts or correct to 2♠.

THE MULTI BY RESPONDER

When partner opens with a minor suit, many players use the bids of 2♡ and 2♠ to show a weak hand. By describing your hand in one bid you make it easy for partner to assess theirs. However, the Multi can be used by responder as well. This approach is rather new and is used nowadays by several top Dutch pairs. The methods described are those developed by Sjoert Brink and Bas Drijver, a pair of young players who are still in their mid-twenties. They have already achieved success on the world stage and play professionally in the United States.

In Brink and Drijver's system, the response of 2♢ after a 1♣ or a 1♢ opening is Multi, showing either a weak two in a major or a game-forcing (14+) hand with diamonds. The idea behind this approach is similar to the Multi 2♢ opening bid: to be able to cover as many hand types as possible. As when opening with a Multi, the bids of 2♡ and 2♠ are now available to show diffent hand types. An extra advantage is that the contract is frequently right-sided. We will come back to that point in a moment.

AFTER A 1♣ OPENING

The response of 2♢ promises either a weak two in a major or a 14+ hand with diamonds:

West	North	East	South
1♣	pass	2♢	

♠KJ9742 ♡104 ♢85 ♣Q75

♠65 ♡QJ10742 ♢1074 ♣82

♠A84 ♡K93 ♢AKJ105 ♣J6

If you are responding as a passed hand, you might agree that your response also promises a degree of fit for partner. For example:

West	North	East	South
		pass	pass
1♣	pass	2♢	

♠ Q J 9 6 4 2 ♡ 6 3 ♢ 2 ♣ 10 9 7 4

That leaves us to decide on the meaning of the responses of 2♡ and 2♠. It is possible to use them as strong game-forcing hands, but in our opinion the frequency of those hand types is very low and it is better to use the bids to show the otherwise awkward intermediate hand types. These would be typical examples:

♠ 8 4 2 ♡ K Q 10 8 6 4 ♢ A 8 4 ♣ 7

♠ A Q J 9 7 3 ♡ 7 6 ♢ J 9 ♣ K 10 4

Opener's Rebid

Opener initially assumes that partner has a weak two in a major and rebids in the Multi style. A rebid of 2♡ suggests that this will be the limit facing a weak two in hearts, 2♠ is to play facing spades (but forward-going opposite hearts) and 2NT is a relay, as after an opening bid of 2♢.

Continuations after Opener Rebids 2♡

West	North	East	South
1♣	pass	2◇	pass
2♡	pass	?	

pass	Weak two in hearts, 2-6 HCP
2♠	Weak two in spades, 2-6 HCP
2NT	Game-forcing with diamonds, 14+ HCP, balanced
3♣	Game-forcing with diamonds and clubs, 14+ HCP
3◇	Game-forcing with diamonds, 14+ HCP, natural
3♡	Game-forcing with diamonds and hearts, 14+ HCP
3♠	Game-forcing with diamonds and spades, 14+ HCP
3NT	Game-forcing with diamonds, 14+ HCP, ugly hand
4♣	Game-forcing with diamonds, 14+ HCP, shortness in clubs
4♡	Game-forcing with diamonds, 14+ HCP, shortness in hearts
4♠	Game-forcing with diamonds, 14+ HCP, shortness in spades

Let's look at a few examples:

♠ 8 4   ♡ A 3   ◇ A Q J 10 7   ♣ K J 7 4

Bid 3♣, game-forcing with diamonds and clubs.

♠ A 9   ♡ K J 7 5   ◇ K Q J 10 8   ♣ 10 6

Bid 3♡, game-forcing with diamonds and hearts.

♠ K Q 10 4   ♡ A 6   ◇ A K 10 9 6 3   ♣ 5

Bid 3♠, game-forcing with diamonds and spades.

♠ Q 10 3   ♡ A J 4   ◇ A K Q J 7 3   ♣ 8

Bid 4♣, game-forcing with diamonds, short clubs.

♠ Q 10 5   ♡ 7   ◇ A K J 10 4 2   ♣ A 7 3

Bid 4♡, game-forcing with diamonds, short hearts.

♠ —   ♡ A K J   ◇ A Q 10 9 5 3 2   ♣ Q 5 2

Bid 4♠, game-forcing with diamonds, short spades.

Continuations after Opener Rebids 2♠

With game interest facing hearts, opener rebids 2♠. For example:

♠ 8   ♡ A 10 5 2   ◇ A Q 3   ♣ K Q 10 9 6

West	North	East	South
1♣	pass	2◇	pass
2♠	pass	?	

pass   *Weak two in spades, 2-6 HCP*
2NT   *Game-forcing with diamonds, 14+ HCP, balanced*
3♣   *Game-forcing with diamonds and clubs, 14+ HCP*
3◇   *Game-forcing with diamonds, 14+ HCP, natural*
3♡   *Hearts, minimum*
3♠   *Game-forcing with diamonds and spades, 14+ HCP*
3NT   *Game-forcing with diamonds, 14+ HCP, ugly hand*
4♣   *Game-forcing with diamonds, 14+ HCP, shortness in clubs*
4♡   *Hearts, maximum*
4♠   *Game-forcing with diamonds, 14+ HCP, shortness in spades*

The 2NT Relay

Opener, with interest in at least a game, may use 2NT as a relay:

♠K 5 ♡A J 3 ◇K 8 2 ♣A Q J 5 2

West	North	East	South
1♣	pass	2◇	pass
2NT	pass	?	

3♣	Weak two in hearts, minimum
3◇	Weak two in spades, minimum
3♡	Weak two in spades, maximum
3♠	Weak two in hearts, maximum (note that this forces the partnership to game, so opener must be prepared for it)
3NT	Diamonds, 14+ HCP, balanced
4♣	Long diamonds and clubs, 14+ HCP
4◇	One-suiter in diamonds, 14+ HCP
4M	One-suiter in diamonds, 14+ HCP, shortness in bid major

AFTER A 1◇ OPENING

West	North	East	South
1◇	pass	2◇	

No strong option is required this time, as all invitational or better hands go via 1◇-2♣, being either balanced, with a diamond fit, or based on clubs. The major-suit bids now become intermediate:

West	North	East	South
1◇	pass	2M	

Six-card suit, 9-11 HCP.

Here is an example from the 2009 Final of the Dutch Premier League, featuring the teams representing De Lombard and 't Onstein, which shows the method in action and illustrates the importance of right-siding the contract:

Both vul.

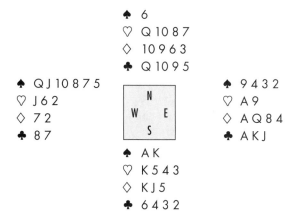

♠ 6
♡ Q 10 8 7
◇ 10 9 6 3
♣ Q 10 9 5

♠ Q J 10 8 7 5
♡ J 6 2
◇ 7 2
♣ 8 7

♠ 9 4 3 2
♡ A 9
◇ A Q 8 4
♣ A K J

♠ A K
♡ K 5 4 3
◇ K J 5
♣ 6 4 3 2

Coincidentally, both East-West pairs were using Multi responses, and in both rooms the bidding went as follows:

West	North	East	South
	pass	1♣	pass
2◇*	pass	2NT*	pass
3◇¹	pass	4♠	all pass

1. Weak two in spades, minimum.

If West declares 4♠, the contract is in serious trouble after a diamond lead. While it can still be made if declarer plays for South to hold king-third of diamonds, it shows how important it is that the contract be played by the strong hand.

CHAPTER 11

THE MULTI IN ACTION

The enormous popularity of the Multi is evidenced in the examples we have selected from play. Here you will find deals involving the strongest players from all over the world. It would have been easy enough only to use examples that show the Multi in a good light, but we have refrained from doing that. Every convention will work perfectly some of the time, but it won't work perfectly all of the time.

One reason why the Multi causes a problem is the fact that opener's suit is unknown. Here is a deal from the final of the Senior teams at the 2008 World Bridge Games:

N-S vul.

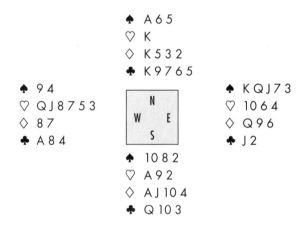

```
                    ♠ A 6 5
                    ♡ K
                    ◇ K 5 3 2
                    ♣ K 9 7 6 5
    ♠ 9 4                              ♠ K Q J 7 3
    ♡ Q J 8 7 5 3        N            ♡ 10 6 4
    ◇ 8 7            W       E        ◇ Q 9 6
    ♣ A 8 4             S             ♣ J 2
                    ♠ 10 8 2
                    ♡ A 9 2
                    ◇ A J 10 4
                    ♣ Q 10 3
```

West	North	East	South
Abe	Lev	Ino	Eisenberg
		pass	pass
2◇*	pass	3♡*	all pass

If West had opened 2♡, North would probably have risked a double, but as it was he felt compelled to pass on the first round and would then have been stretching on the next. Meanwhile, 3NT is a playable contract for North-South and it was made at the other table.

Here is another example from the Open event at the same tournament:

N-S vul.

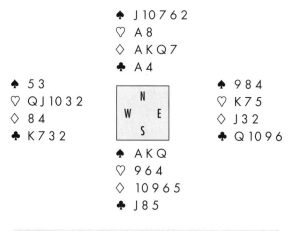

West	North	East	South
Groetheim	Lauria	Tundal	Versace
2◊*	dbl	3♡*	3NT
all pass			

The cramping effect of East's raise gave one of the world's best pairs no room to maneuver. Still, we hear you say, it is impossible to reach 6◊ even if you know West has hearts. Actually, this was the auction in another match:

West	North	East	South
Hackett	Gromoeller	Hackett	Kirmse
2♡	dbl	3♡	dbl
pass	4♡	pass	5◊
pass	6◊	all pass	

When South made a negative double over 3♡, North showed his extra values and then raised his partner's suit.

When responder has a fit for both majors he can put the pressure on with a preemptive jump, as we saw in the previous example. Here is another one from the 2008 World Bridge Games:

N-S vul.

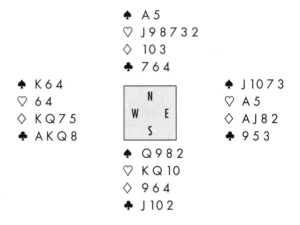

             ♠ A 5
             ♡ J 9 8 7 3 2
             ◇ 10 3
             ♣ 7 6 4

♠ K 6 4   ♠ J 10 7 3
♡ 6 4   ♡ A 5
◇ K Q 7 5   ◇ A J 8 2
♣ A K Q 8   ♣ 9 5 3

             ♠ Q 9 8 2
             ♡ K Q 10
             ◇ 9 6 4
             ♣ J 10 2

West	North	East	South
Houmoller	*Nawrocki*	*Schaltz*	*Sikora*
	2◇*	pass	3♡*
dbl	pass	**4♠**	all pass

North's somewhat daring vulnerable Multi eventually left East with a guess — should he bid 3NT or 4♠? When he guessed to try the ten-trick game, repeated heart leads meant he had to go one down. Yes, they did reach 3NT at the other table.

A common problem for responder is what to do with an intermediate hand, which might offer a chance of game if partner's hand is suitable. This deal from the 2005 final of the Dutch Premier League between De Lombard and Modalfa is a good example:

Neither vul.

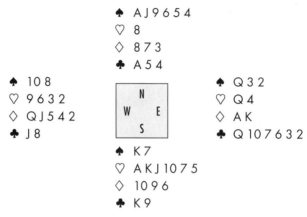

♠ A J 9 6 5 4
♡ 8
◇ 8 7 3
♣ A 5 4

♠ 10 8
♡ 9 6 3 2
◇ Q J 5 4 2
♣ J 8

♠ Q 3 2
♡ Q 4
◇ A K
♣ Q 10 7 6 3 2

♠ K 7
♡ A K J 10 7 5
◇ 10 9 6
♣ K 9

West	North	East	South
Nab	Drijver	Paulissen	Schollaardt
pass	2◇*	pass	2♡*
pass	2♠	pass	2NT
pass	3NT	all pass	

Maarten Schollaardt as South anticipated a weak two in spades and therefore opted for a non-forcing 2♡ response. In the unlikely case that Bas Drijver had a weak two in hearts, East-West would possess a huge fit in spades and probably win the auction anyway. After the expected 2♠ rebid, South launched a mild game try with 2NT. This worked out well when North, with an outside stopper, raised to game. Due to the blockage in diamonds the contract was an easy make, but even with diamonds 4-3, 3NT has many chances.

One factor that must always be taken into account is that when a Multi is opened, the major suit it is based on is unknown. Here is an example from the 2001 Cap Gemini World Pairs in The Hague:

Geir Helgemo

Both vul.

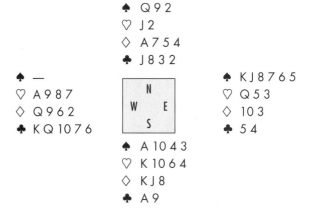

West	North	East	South
Helgemo	Robson	Forrester	Zia
		2◊*	2NT
pass	3NT	pass	pass
dbl	all pass		

It is interesting to notice that Tony Forrester, even though vulnerable, opted for the aggressive approach by opening a Multi on very light values and was not deterred from doing so by holding queen-third in the other major. Geir Helgemo could see that North-South were bidding on thin values and therefore doubled for penalties.

Zia Mahmood had no clue which major East had, which made it difficult to make a sensible plan as declarer, and he finished up going down two.

The fact that the Multi suit is unknown can produce some surprising results, as on this deal from the final at the 2006 European Bridge Champions' Cup, played between Bamberg, representing Germany, and De Lombard from The Netherlands:

E-W vul.

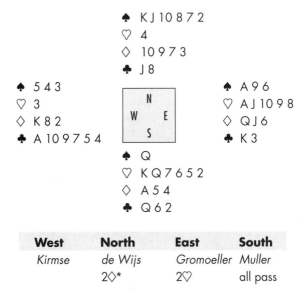

```
              ♠ K J 10 8 7 2
              ♡ 4
              ◇ 10 9 7 3
              ♣ J 8
  ♠ 5 4 3                        ♠ A 9 6
  ♡ 3            N               ♡ A J 10 9 8
  ◇ K 8 2    W       E           ◇ Q J 6
  ♣ A 10 9 7 5 4     S           ♣ K 3
              ♠ Q
              ♡ K Q 7 6 5 2
              ◇ A 5 4
              ♣ Q 6 2
```

West	North	East	South
Kirmse	*de Wijs*	*Gromoeller*	*Muller*
	2◇*	2♡	all pass

Facing an overcall of North's Multi, West was not prepared to enter the fray. Perhaps East should have simply overcalled 2NT, which at least gets the general strength of his hand across. It would have then been possible for West to search for a 5-3 spade fit if he was so inclined. Declarer was able to make his contract, but the thin 3NT was bid and made in the other room after a 2♠ opening from North.

Clearly, when the Multi is overcalled it can be a problem knowing what to lead. American expert Kit Woolsey has done some work on this and come up with an interesting idea. Sitting East at favorable vulnerability, you have this hand:

♠K 5   ♡A 7 3   ◇K 8   ♣9 8 6 5 3 2

You have to find a lead after this auction:

West	North	East	South
partner		you	
2◇*	2NT	pass	3NT
all pass			

It is obvious that your choice is between the ♠K or the ♡3. Since you don't know your partner's long major, you have a 50% chance of picking the wrong suit.

When hearts is partner's long suit there is a good chance that 3NT is going down. But how can you know that? Kit Woolsey has found a solution for this problem. The answer is to bid 3♣ yourself over 2NT. This asks partner to double with long hearts if advancer raises to 3NT. Similarly, bidding 3◇ asks partner to double 3NT when his long suit is spades. In other words, three in a minor by the Multi responder is pass-or-correct to three of opener's major. This method requires good timing, as sometimes it means your side will have to play at the three-level.

Here is an example from the Jacoby Open Swiss Teams, played at the Spring Nationals in Houston in 2009. With neither vulnerable and North dealer, Steve Robinson (South) had this hand:

♠A Q 2   ♡9 5 4   ◇Q J 9 8 2   ♣7 4

West	North	East	South
Rodwell	Boyd	Meckstroth	Robinson
	2◇*	2NT	3◇[1]
3NT	pass[2]	all pass	

1. Asking partner to double 3NT when he has long spades.
2. North's long suit was hearts.

So Robinson led a heart, which beat the contract. This was the complete
deal:

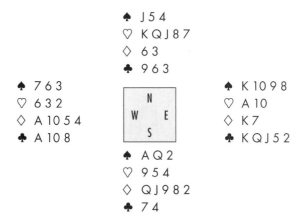

```
                    ♠ J 5 4
                    ♡ K Q J 8 7
                    ◇ 6 3
                    ♣ 9 6 3
  ♠ 7 6 3                               ♠ K 10 9 8
  ♡ 6 3 2           N                   ♡ A 10
  ◇ A 10 5 4    W       E               ◇ K 7
  ♣ A 10 8          S                   ♣ K Q J 5 2
                    ♠ A Q 2
                    ♡ 9 5 4
                    ◇ Q J 9 8 2
                    ♣ 7 4
```

Steve Robinson

A recurring theme is that responder may sometimes be pleasantly surprised when opener reveals which suit they have, as on this example from the match between Egypt and Russia in the 2005 World Championships in Estoril:

N-S vul.

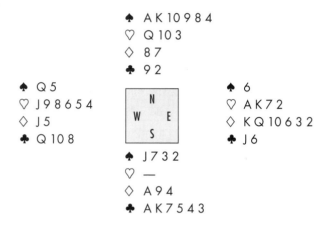

```
                    ♠ A K 10 9 8 4
                    ♡ Q 10 3
                    ◇ 8 7
                    ♣ 9 2
  ♠ Q 5                              ♠ 6
  ♡ J 9 8 6 5 4         N            ♡ A K 7 2
  ◇ J 5            W         E       ◇ K Q 10 6 3 2
  ♣ Q 10 8             S            ♣ J 6
                    ♠ J 7 3 2
                    ♡ —
                    ◇ A 9 4
                    ♣ A K 7 5 4 3
```

Open room

West	North	East	South
Kholomeev	El Ahmady	Zlotov	Sadek
pass	2◇*	pass	2♡*
pass	2♠	dbl	pass
4♡	pass	pass	4♠
pass	pass	dbl	all pass

South must have been surprised when his partner's suit turned out to be spades. As an aside, we would not recommend passing 2◇ with the East hand — an immediate overcall of 3◇ is in order. In one match where East overcalled 2◇ with 3◇, that ended the auction — the downside of not knowing which suit opener has! West's jump to 4♡ was aggressive and apparently when 4♠ was doubled, South assumed the expression of a man about to mount the scaffold! The outcome was +1390 for North-South.

Tarek Sadek

We should mention that once the suit has been revealed an inspired opponent may be able to make use of the information, as in this example from the 2006 Juno Cup in Wuxi, China:

N-S vul.

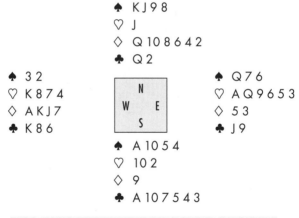

West	North	East	South
Gromann	*Wortel*	*Weber*	*Michielsen*
	pass	2◇*	pass
2♠*	pass	3♡	pass
4♡	pass	pass	4♠(!)
dbl	all pass		

After East-West reached the heart game, the bidding seemed to have come to an end. Not so with Marion Michielsen at the table. As South she made the daring bid of 4♠, vulnerable against not, on only a four-card spade suit (Marshall Miles would surely approve!).

From the bidding, Michielsen concluded that her opponents had a huge heart fit with not that many points and not that many spades. Therefore her partner was bound to have a good hand for spades and some points as well. Moreover, Michielsen did not run to 5♣ but confidently passed when she was doubled.

Double dummy, 4♠ can be defeated, but in practice when the smoke cleared, North-South were +790.

This deal is a clear example of how carefully the 2♠ relay should be treated. The bid might help the opponents enormously, in both the bidding and play. If West had begun with a 2♡ relay, essentially giving up on the idea of a possible game in hearts, it is not at all certain that North-South would have reached the spade game.

Marion Michielsen

Experience has shown that it can be advantageous to open a Multi even with a five-card suit. This next example is taken from the round robin phase of the 2006 Dutch Premier League, when the two teams representing 't Onstein faced off across the table:

N-S vul.

```
                    ♠ J 10 3
                    ♡ A 6 4 2
                    ◇ K Q 6
                    ♣ A 10 9
    ♠ 8 7                              ♠ A K Q 4
    ♡ K Q J 10 8         N            ♡ 7 3
    ◇ 9 2           W         E       ◇ A J 10 8 4 3
    ♣ Q 6 3 2           S            ♣ K
                    ♠ 9 6 5 2
                    ♡ 9 5
                    ◇ 7 5
                    ♣ J 8 7 5 4
```

West	North	East	South
van Munnen	Verhees	Ritmeijer	Jansma
			pass
2◇*	dbl[1]	pass[2]	2♠
pass	pass	dbl	all pass

1. 12-14 bal. or a strong hand.
2. Long diamonds.

As in most versions of the Multi, East-West were willing to open on a five-card suit. East was almost certain that his partner's weak two was in hearts. But he didn't bid them. On the contrary, Richard Ritmeijer did something much smarter: he passed. In view of his diamond holding he could freely do so. East foresaw that he might well be able to double his vulnerable opponents for penalties on the next round, which is exactly what happened.

Two spades was a catastrophe. With accurate defense declarer will only make three tricks, two aces and a trump, and East-West did indeed record +1400. The deal is just another example where even a world-class player like Jan Jansma sometimes takes the wrong view defending against a Multi auction. Notice that over a weak two-bid in hearts, North-South would not have entered the bidding, and if West had passed initially North's opening bid of 1♣ would have seen East overcall.

In the previous example, West's Multi suit was very robust, even though it only contained five cards. However, some pairs are more than happy to base their opening bid on something much more flimsy, as on this deal from the 1991 Cap Gemini Pan Data World Pairs in The Hague:

Jeff Meckstroth

E-W vul.

```
              ♠ A K
              ♡ 9 4
              ◇ Q 9 7 2
              ♣ A K 6 4 3
  ♠ 6                          ♠ J 8 7 4 3
  ♡ K J 8 7 3 2       N        ♡ A Q 10
  ◇ K             W       E    ◇ J 10 8 3
  ♣ J 10 9 8 2        S        ♣ 5
              ♠ Q 10 9 5 2
              ♡ 6 5
              ◇ A 6 5 4
              ♣ Q 7
```

West	North	East	South
Terraneo	Meckstroth	Fucik	Rodwell
			2◇*
pass	2♡*	pass	2♠
all pass			

In spite of his 16 HCP North did not consider his hand to be invitational. Jeff Meckstroth had two good reasons for this careful approach. Firstly, in Meckwell style, at favorable colors a Multi opening usually has more preemptive then constructive character, so South could be very weak. Secondly, the weak two might well be based on only a five-card suit.

In the spade partscore Eric Rodwell made nine tricks, though with best defense eight tricks is the maximum. Not that it mattered much, as at all other tables either North-South went down in 3NT or 4♠ or East-West made a (doubled) heart contract. In that regard it is interesting to see that Franz Terraneo refrained from overcalling with the West hand.

In the following case from the 2008 World Bridge Games Womens' Final in Beijing between China and England, the player in the East seat was not prepared to venture a five-card Multi — but that was not the whole story:

N-S vul.

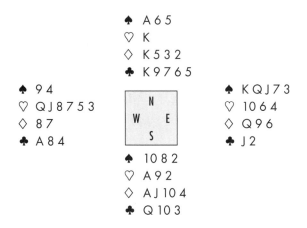

```
                  ♠ A 6 5
                  ♡ K
                  ◇ K 5 3 2
                  ♣ K 9 7 6 5
  ♠ 9 4                              ♠ K Q J 7 3
  ♡ Q J 8 7 5 3         N            ♡ 10 6 4
  ◇ 8 7           W           E      ◇ Q 9 6
  ♣ A 8 4              S             ♣ J 2
                  ♠ 10 8 2
                  ♡ A 9 2
                  ◇ A J 10 4
                  ♣ Q 10 3
```

West	North	East	South
Wang	Draper	Sun	Rosen
		pass	pass
2◇*	pass	3♡*	all pass

North had no convenient way into the auction on the first round and then had to guess on the next after East's preemptive action. The singleton ♡K appeared to be of dubious value and her main suit was hardly robust — she decided to pass. South led a trump and thereafter declarer was easily held to six tricks, -150. Meanwhile, bidding and making 3NT on the North-South cards is quite possible if West opens 2♡.

We imagine everyone is familiar with the principle that a hand which has taken a preemptive action does not bid again, but when the Multi is in operation the bidding may develop in such a way that some further action suggests itself, as on this deal from the 2006 Modalfa Top 12 in Amsterdam:

```
               ♠ —
               ♡ K 10 6 3 2
               ◇ A K 6 3
               ♣ A K 4 3
  ♠ A K J 8 4 2        ┌─────────┐        ♠ Q 10
  ♡ J 4               │    N    │         ♡ Q 9 8 5
  ◇ 10 9 4            │  W   E  │         ◇ Q 8 7 2
  ♣ 7 2               │    S    │         ♣ Q 9 6
                       └─────────┘
               ♠ 9 7 6 5 3
               ♡ A 7
               ◇ J 5
               ♣ J 10 8 5
```

West	North	East	South
De Wijs	Drijver	Muller	Brink
			pass
2◇*	dbl	2♡*	2♠
pass	2NT	pass	3NT
dbl	all pass		

Over West's Multi North had a dilemma: should he overcall in hearts (despite his modest suit and many HCPs in the two other suits) or should he double, despite the spade void? Bas Drijver opted for the latter. As a result the partnership was in muddy waters, especially when the Multi opener, Simon de Wijs, launched a Lightner double, demanding a lead in dummy's suit. Against 3NT doubled Bauke Muller led the ♠Q. West contributed the eight — suit preference — and East duly switched to a low heart. There was no way declarer could avoid down two.

Let's have a look at another table were North did overcall 2♡:

West	North	East	South
Hop	Van Prooijen	Ter Laare	Eskes
			pass
2◇*	2♡	2♠	pass
pass	dbl	pass	3♡
pass	4♡	dbl	all pass

When East's 2♠ came back to him, North was in a good position to keep the bidding alive with a takeout double. Over 3♡, Ricco van Prooijen aggressively pushed himself to game. While not laydown, 4♡ was playable and declarer did indeed end up with ten tricks.

Another possible reason for the Multi opener to take a second unforced bid might be extreme distribution, as on this deal from the match between Norway and the Netherlands at the 2005 World Championships in Estoril:

Both vul.

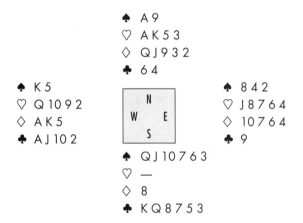

```
              ♠ A 9
              ♡ A K 5 3
              ◇ Q J 9 3 2
              ♣ 6 4
♠ K 5                          ♠ 8 4 2
♡ Q 10 9 2         N          ♡ J 8 7 6 4
◇ A K 5        W       E      ◇ 10 7 6 4
♣ A J 10 2         S          ♣ 9
              ♠ Q J 10 7 6 3
              ♡ —
              ◇ 8
              ♣ K Q 8 7 5 3
```

West	North	East	South
Brogeland	Wijs	Saelensminde	Muller
			2◇*
2NT	pass	3◇*	4♣
4♡	dbl	all pass	

Muller did not adopt a waiting game, showing a major and then bidding again to indicate his extreme distribution over East's transfer to hearts. When West went on to game (how could he possibly pass?) North must have been delighted. The result was down three, -800. However, East-West had the last laugh, as their partners were extracting 1100 from 3◇ doubled at the other table.

The current rules regarding the use of the Multi in North America mean that players from that continent are afforded little opportunity to play against it. Being on unfamiliar ground can cause problems, as on this deal from the 2008 Transnational Championship in Beijing:

E-W vul.

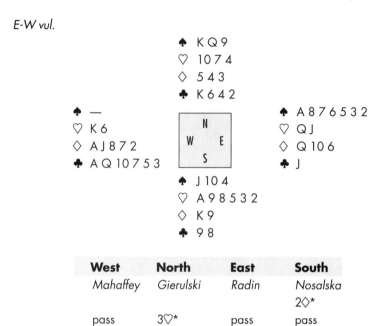

	♠ K Q 9	
	♡ 10 7 4	
	◇ 5 4 3	
	♣ K 6 4 2	
♠ —		♠ A 8 7 6 5 3 2
♡ K 6	N	♡ Q J
◇ A J 8 7 2	W E	◇ Q 10 6
♣ A Q 10 7 5 3	S	♣ J
	♠ J 10 4	
	♡ A 9 8 5 3 2	
	◇ K 9	
	♣ 9 8	

West	North	East	South
Mahaffey	*Gierulski*	*Radin*	*Nosalska*
			2◇*
pass	3♡*	pass	pass
3NT*	pass	4◇	all pass

Over the preemptive 3♡, 3NT promised both minors, but East decided she did not have enough to bid game. She made eleven tricks, +150. At the other table West made a more effective immediate entry into the auction with 4NT, which forced his side to the making game.

With a fit for both majors responder can compete for the partscore even after the opening bid has been overcalled, as on this deal from the match between Italy and Sweden at the 2005 World Championships in Estoril:

N-S vul.

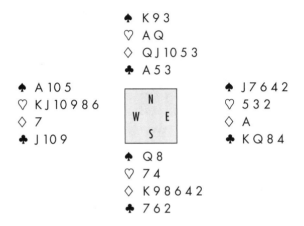

```
                    ♠ K 9 3
                    ♡ A Q
                    ◇ Q J 10 5 3
                    ♣ A 5 3
  ♠ A 10 5                          ♠ J 7 6 4 2
  ♡ K J 10 9 8 6        N           ♡ 5 3 2
  ◇ 7              W         E       ◇ A
  ♣ J 10 9             S            ♣ K Q 8 4
                    ♠ Q 8
                    ♡ 7 4
                    ◇ K 9 8 6 4 2
                    ♣ 7 6 2
```

Open room

West	North	East	South
Sylvan	Fantoni	Sundelin	Nunes
		pass	pass
2◇*	2NT	3♡*	all pass

A slight defensive error saw declarer emerge with ten tricks, +170.

In the early days of preemptive bidding it was considered to be a crime to hold four cards in an unbid major. Nowadays experts frequently have a different view, as on this deal from the match between Norway and the Netherlands at the 1993 European Championships in Menton:

Berry Westra

Neither vul.

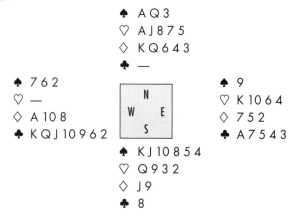

♠ A Q 3
♥ A J 8 7 5
♦ K Q 6 4 3
♣ —

♠ 7 6 2
♥ —
♦ A 10 8
♣ K Q J 10 9 6 2

♠ 9
♥ K 10 6 4
♦ 7 5 2
♣ A 7 5 4 3

♠ K J 10 8 5 4
♥ Q 9 3 2
♦ J 9
♣ 8

West	North	East	South
Grøtheim	Westra	Aa	Leufkens
			2◊*
3♣	4♡*	5♣	pass
pass	5◊	pass	5♠
all pass			

Enri Leufkens considered his six-card spade suit too good to contemplate passing, despite the presence of four hearts. With his jump to 4♡, Berry Westra showed a willingness to play in his partner's weak two at the four-level. On the next round Westra bid again — give South the ◊A and even slam is on. With diamonds 3-3 there was nothing to the play in 5♠, and Leufkens made twelve tricks.

When this next deal came up in the closing stages of the 2009 World Championships every player in the East seat with the right club in their bag opened with just about the weakest Multi you will ever see — and for several of them it brought a huge reward:

N-S vul.

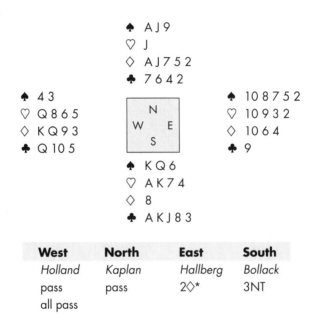

♠ A J 9
♡ J
◇ A J 7 5 2
♣ 7 6 4 2

♠ 4 3
♡ Q 8 6 5
◇ K Q 9 3
♣ Q 10 5

♠ 10 8 7 5 2
♡ 10 9 3 2
◇ 10 6 4
♣ 9

♠ K Q 6
♡ A K 7 4
◇ 8
♣ A K J 8 3

West	North	East	South
Holland	*Kaplan*	*Hallberg*	*Bollack*
pass	pass	2◇*	3NT
all pass			

When South jumped to 3NT, North was no doubt tempted to do something. When he passed, scoring ten tricks on a spade lead, England picked up 12 IMPs for the club slam bid at the other table. If North had decided to bid, one idea is to adopt whatever method you would have used over a 2♣ opening and 3NT rebid, one possibility being 4♣ Stayman, 4◇/4♡ transfers and 4♠ for the minors.

Finally, it pays not to push the opponents too high when you have little defense: sometimes you get what you wish for! This deal came up in the 2009 World Championships in Sao Paulo, Brazil. This auction is from the Venice Cup match between China and Sweden.

E-W vul.

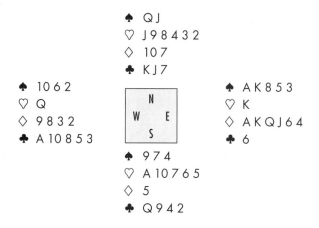

	♠ Q J	
	♡ J 9 8 4 3 2	
	◇ 10 7	
	♣ K J 7	
♠ 10 6 2		♠ A K 8 5 3
♡ Q		♡ K
◇ 9 8 3 2		◇ A K Q J 6 4
♣ A 10 8 5 3		♣ 6
	♠ 9 7 4	
	♡ A 10 7 6 5	
	◇ 5	
	♣ Q 9 4 2	

West	North	East	South
S. Rimstedt	Sun	Sjoberg	Wang Hongli
			pass
pass	2◇*	dbl	3♡*
pass	pass	4♡¹	pass
5♣*	pass	5◇	all pass

1. Leaping Michaels.

In the Open Room, vigorous preemption pushed Wang Wenfei into bidding 6◇. True, looking at only the East-West cards, the slam seems to have two losers, one heart and one spade. But then you peek at the North hand and see that queen-jack doubleton of spades.

In the Multi auction Wang Hongli did well. If she had bid three spades, North would have rebid four hearts. Then East might have bid five hearts, getting to the poor but making slam.

APPENDIX — THE KOKISH 'SIMPLE' DEFENSE TO MULTI

DEFENSE VS. 2◇ MULTI: WEAK 2M, WITH/WITHOUT STRONG OPTION(S)

Directly over 2◇:

Pass	Neutral, OR takeout DBL of one M, or decent but not FG two-suiter
DBL	14-16+ or 20+ (bid again) BAL, or sound 18+ UNBAL
2NT	17-19 (3♣=Stayman, 3◇/♡=transfer, 3♠=minors)
2M	NAT (2NT F1, cheap OM=ART, jump OM=NAT); Responsive DBLs
3♣	NAT (3◇=ART, 3M NAT); Responsive DBLs
3◇	NAT (3♠ NAT, 3♡=♡ or ♡ guard [then 3♠=OK for ♡: resp's 3NT=♡ guard/other=♡]); Resp DBL
3♡*	5+m/5+♡, FG (over 3♡: 3NT=NAT; 3♠ asks: 3N=♣/4♣=◇/4♡=6+♡; 4♣=slam try in minor; 4◇=slam try in ♡)
3♠*	5+m/5+♠, FG (over 3♠: 3NT=NAT; 4♣ asks: 4◇=♣/4♡=◇/4♠=6+♠; 4◇=slam try in minor; 4♡=slam try in spades)
3NT	NAT, tricks (transfer advances)
4m*	5+m/5+M, NF (over 4m: cheapest=slam try in M; next non-4NT=slam try in a minor; 4NT=6 RKCB)
4M	Strong (cheap step RKCB1430-M, others: controls agreeing M/4NT over 4♡=♠ control)
4NT*	Minors, sound

NOTE: For 4m, you might have: KQ10xx, x, AQJ10xx, x (4◇); 3M overcalls are strong 5/5+ hands.

Developments:

West	North	East	South
(2◇)	pass	(2♡*)	

Pass   NF (later: DBL ♠= T/O, 2NT=2-suiter, 3x NAT/
            limited)

DBL   Takeout of ♡ (LEB advances)

2♠   NAT (2NT/3m= F1, 3♡=ART, 4♡=SPL);

2NT   15-18 (3♣=Stayman, 3◇/♡=transfer, 3♠=minors)

3♣   NAT (3◇=ART, 3M NAT, 4M=SPL, 4◇=FIT)

3◇   NAT (3♠ NAT, 3♡=♡ or ♡ stop [3♠=OK for ♡: resp's
            3NT=♡ stop/else=♡])

3♡*   5+m/5+♡, FG (3N=NAT; 4♣/4◇=SLAM TRY in m/♡;
            3♠=?; 3N=♣/4♣=◇/4♡=6+♡)

3♠*   5+m/5+♠, FG (3N=NAT; 4◇/4♡=SLAM TRY in m/♠;
            4 ♣=?: 4◇=♣/4♡=◇/4♠=6+♠)

3NT   NAT, tricks (transfer advances)

4m*   5+m/5+♡, NF (cheapest=slam try ♡; next non-
            4NT=slam try in a minor; 4NT=6RKCB)

4M   Strong (cheap=RKCB1430-M, else controls for
            M/4NT over 4♡=♠ control)

4NT*   Minors, sound

West	North	East	South
(2◇)	pass	(2♠*)	

Pass   NF (later: DBL ♡= T/O, 2NT=2-suiter, 3x NAT/
            limited)

DBL   Takeout of ♠ (LEB advances)

2NT   15-18 (3♣=Stayman, 3◇/♡=transfer, 3♠=minors)

3♣   NAT (3◇=ART, 3M NAT, 4M=SPL, 4◇=FIT)

3◇   NAT (3♠ NAT, 3♡=♡ or ♡ stop [3♠=OK for ♡: resp's
            3NT=♡ stop/else=♡])

3♡*   5+m/5+♡, FG (3N=NAT; 4♣/4◇=slam try in a
            minor/♡; 3♠=?: 3N=♣/4♣=◇/4♡=6+♡)

3♠*   5+m/5+♠, FG (3N=NAT; 4◇/4♡=slam try in a
            minor/♠; 4♣=?: 4◇=♣/4♡=◇/4♠=6+♠)

3NT   NAT, tricks (transfer advances)
4m*   5+m/5+♠, NF (cheapest=slam try in hearts; next non-
         4NT=slam try in a minor; 4NT=6 RKCB)
4M   Strong (cheap=RKCB 1430-M, else controls for
         M/4NT over 4♡=♠ control)
4NT*   Minors, sound

West	North	East	South
(2◇)	pass	(2M)*	pass
(P/2♠)			

DBL   Takeout, could be full value (LEB advances)
2NT   ♣+◇ (but over 2♠ either ♣+♡ or ◇+♡ possible)
Cue   4OM/6+m, fair hand
Suit bids   NAT (limited by failure to act over 2◇)

West	North	East	South
(2◇)	pass	(3M/4M)*	

Pass   NF (later double of correction = takeout)
DBL   Takeout
3NT   NAT, covers a lot of ground (4♣ asks TYPE/TFR
         advances)
Others   NAT

West	North	East	South
(2◇)	pass	(3♡/4♡)*	pass
(pass)			

DBL   Takeout
3♠/4♠*   5+♠/5+m, limited hand
3NT/4NT*   ♣+◇
4♡*   4♠/6m, fair hand
Others   Less than immediate suit bids (not very likely)

West	North	East	South
(2◊)	pass	(3♠)*	pass
(P)			

DBL   Takeout
3NT*   Two-suiter (pass-or-correct technique when advancing)
4♡*   Lots of ♡, not a great hand, counting on partner for
       cards
Others Less than immediate suit bids (not very likely)
4NT   ♣+◊ (stronger than 3NT*)

West	North	East	South
(2◊)	pass	(4m*)	

DBL   Like a sound overcall in that suit (where 4m is
       artificial)
Double of 4M later = takeout

West	North	East	South
(2◊)	pass	(4m*)	pass
(4M)			

DBL   Takeout

West	North	East	South
(2◊)	pass	(2NT=INQ)	

DBL   STR at least 4/3 Ms
3x   NAT
3NT   Tricks
4M   STR
4m   5+m/5+M, FG

West	North	East	South
(2◊)	pass	(pass)*	
	*[where pass is random or shows ◊]		

DBL   *Takeout of ◊ or very strong*
2M   *NAT*
2NT   *About 15-18 (normal agreements to advance)*
3♣   *NAT (3◊=ART, 3M=NAT)*
3◊*   *Some solid suit, no ◊ guard*
3M   *STR*
3NT   *Tricks*
4♣*   *5+♣/5+♡, FG*
4◊*   *5+♣/5+♠, FG*

West	North	East	South
(2◊)	DBL	(2♡)*	

2♠   *NAT, NF: theoretically 5+♠ as DBL suggests 2+♠*

West	North	East	South
(2◊)	DBL	(2M)*	

Pass   *NF: then DBL of CORRECTION is for takeout*
DBL*   *Responsive, at least INV strength, some defensive tolerance*
2NT*   *Lebensohl: weak ANY suit, or FG with ♣*
3♣*   *Stayman, FG: typically 41 or 14 in the majors (else DBL)*
3◊/3M   *NAT, FG*
3NT   *Stoppers in both Ms, about 11-15 HCP*
4m   *NAT, FG, one-suited with slam interest*
4M/4OM   *NAT, distributional*
4NT   *Blackwood, aces*

If they bid 3M/4M as P/C: new suits are FG, 4M over their 3M is NAT; 4NT= RKCB over 3M, NAT over 4M, Responsive DBLS

West	North	East	South
(2◇)	DBL	(2M)*	

2NT*   *Lebensohl (not strong [unless with ♣], but some values, else pass over 2M)*

3♣*   *14-16 BAL (with "more" doubler does otherwise)*

3◇*   *ART, 20+ BAL FG (then NAT bidding)*

3M   *NAT, 18+, UNBAL, GF (then: OM is a cue bid, 4m is NAT)*

3NT   *NAT, strong, 22(54), so advancer knows what to do with only 5M*

West	North	East	South
(2◇)	DBL	(2M)*	2NT*
(pass)	3♣*	(pass)	

Pass   *Our route to 3♣*

3◇   *Our route to 3◇*

3♡*   *GF with ♣ (plus 4♡); i.e. NAT*

3♠*   *GF with ♣ (plus 4♠), i.e. NAT*

3NT   *GF with ♣ (one-suiter)*

If memory strain is not an issue 3♡ could show 4♠, 3♠ could show 4♡

West	North	East	South
(2◇)	DBL	(2M)*	pass
(P/2♠)			

DBL   *20+, cooperative takeout (LEB advances)*

SUIT   *NAT, 18+ UNBAL*

West	North	East	South
(2◇)	DBL	(P/RDBL)	
	[where pass or RDBL is neutral or shows ◇]		

Pass	*Willing to defend, but might not be big ◇ stack*
2M	*NAT, COMP strength, may be scramble if unable to defend*
2NT*	*Lebensohl (♣: COMP or FG — 3NT or 3M [4M/5+♣] next)*
3♣*	*Stayman, typically 41 or 14 in the majors*
3◇*	*Asks for ◇ stopper (we just pass with ◇)*
3M	*NAT, FG*
3NT	*NAT, about 11-15, major suit stoppers*
4♣	*NAT, slam try*
4◇/4♡*	*Texas (then 4M+1=RKC, others=Exclusion)*
4♠*	*RKCB♣*
4NT	*Blackwood, aces*

West	North	East	South
(2◇)	DBL	(2♡)*	DBL*
(P)			

Pass	*Good defense*
2♠	*4♠ (but NOT both maximum AND a ♡ stopper)*
2NT	*NAT, non-maximum*
3m	*NAT, non maximum*
3♡*	*Max, 4♠ plus a ♡ stopper (3♠ forces 3NT; 4♡ forces 4♠) OR 20+ BAL or SEMI-BAL (bid again)*
3♠*	*Maximum, not 4♠, no ♡ stopper OR 20+ BAL (bid again)*
3NT	*Maximum, not 4♠, but has a ♡ stopper*
4m/4♠	*NAT, 20+ (now 4NT is NAT)*
4♡*	*Huge three-suiter*

West	North	East	South
(2◊)	DBL	(2♡)*	DBL*
(2♠)			

Pass	NF (reopening: DBL=PEN, 3♠=FG w/ SPL ♠)
DBL	PEN (takeout to 3♠=FG w/ SPL ♠)
2NT	NAT, non-minimum
3m	NAT, non-minimum
3♡	NAT, 18+ FG, probably only five hearts
3♠	Maximum, no ♠ stopper, or 20+ BAL (bid again)
3NT	NAT, expecting a minimum of 9 HCP
4m/4♡	NAT, 20+ (now 4NT = NAT over 4m, RKCB over 4♡)
4♠*	Huge three-suiter

West	North	East	South
(2◊)	DBL	(2♠)*	DBL*
(P)			

Pass	Good defense
2NT	NAT, non-maximum
3m/3♡	NAT, non-maximum
3♠*	Maximum, no ♠ stopper OR 20+ BAL (bid again)
3NT	Maximum, NAT
4m/4♡	NAT, 20+ (now 4NT is NAT)
4♠*	Huge three-suiter

West	North	East	South
(2◊)	DBL	(2♠)*	DBL*
(3♡)			

Pass	NF (reopening DBL=PEN, 3♠=FG, no ♡ stopper; 3NT NAT)
DBL	PEN (takeout to 3♠ unlikely, probably ♣+◊ length, 3NT NAT)
3♠	NAT, 18+ FG, probably only five spades
3NT	NAT, expecting a minimum of 9 HCP
4m/4♠	NAT, 20+ (now 4NT = NAT over 4m, RKCB over 4♠)
4♡*	Huge three-suiter

West	North	East	South
(2◇)	DBL	(3♣)	

Pass   NF
DBL*   Responsive (cooperative takeout)
3◇*   ♡ INV+ TFR (3♠*=cue, looking for club stopper)
3♡*   ♠ INV+ TFR
3♠*   ◇ INV+ TFR (FG unless doubler bids 4◇)
3NT   NAT (♣ stopper)
4♣   5+♡/5+◇, slam try
4◇   5+♠/5+◇, slam try

If that looks like memory strain, revert to NAT. Sure to be a low frequency auction.

West	North	East	South
(2◇)	DBL	(3◇)	

Pass   NF
DBL*   Responsive (cooperative takeout)
3M   FG (perhaps a stretch)
3NT   NAT (◇ stopper)
4♣   INV
4◇/♡* TRF to ♡/♠
4♠*   TRF to ♣, FG

West	North	East	South
(2◇)	DBL	(3♡)*	

Pass   NF (later: DBL of ♠ correction for takeout, bid 4♡ NAT)
DBL*   Responsive (cooperative takeout)
3♠   FG (perhaps a stretch)
3NT   NAT
4m   NAT, INV
4♡*   TRF to ♠
4♠*   TRF to ♣
4NT*   TRF to ◇

West	North	East	South
(2♢)	DBL	(3♠*)	

Pass NF (later: DBL of ♡ correction for takeout, bid 4♠
   NAT)

DBL* Responsive (cooperative takeout)

3NT NAT (♡ stopper most important)

4♣ NAT, INV

4♢* TRF to ♡

4♡* TRF to ♣

4♠* TRF to ♢ (no INV 4♢ available)